T0279503

Playing to Learn

Using **IMPROV**
in the K-8 Classroom

Kate Wiersema

ISBN 979-8-35094-385-6

eBook ISBN 979-8-35094-386-3

Contents

Author's Note

As teachers, we know that no new ideas exist. We "borrow" lessons and ideas all the time. The same is true in the world of improv. Only about six basic games exist; everything else is a version of one of them. Throughout my ten plus years of improv experience, I have stolen, borrowed, modified, changed, and created many games. I want to thank all of the organizations and people I have had the pleasure of playing with for inspiration for the book. Some of these include, but are not limited to: Improductions LLC, South of Chi Productions, No Limit Laughs Improv, and Malarkey Comedy (ComedySportz Chicago). I intend no ill will if I have taken a game that you created or taught me and changed it to work within the classroom. As I tell my kids all the time, once you learn a game, it is yours. My hope is that through learning these games, teachers will be inspired to modify them for their specific lessons and individual students.

This book is dedicated to Eric and my Mom and Dad. Here is your Anderson Theory.

Introduction

When you walked across the stage to receive your degree in education, what thoughts went through your head? "I can't wait to build relationships with students!" "My classroom is going to be like Ms. Honey's room from *Matilda*; no one will ever want to leave!" "You know the Golden Apple Award? They are going to have to make the PLATINUM Apple by the time I am done with this profession!"

Now... fast forward 5, 10, 30 years. What do you see in your head when you think of your classroom? Standardized tests, a to-do list that never ends, and that kid that keeps putting everything in his mouth? (Yes, Derek... we all notice and it is gross.)

What if we could rewind back to the time when you were excited to see your kids and they were excited to, *GASP*, be in school? We always have the passion and the want to build those relationships, teach meaningful lessons, and have fun while doing it; but sometimes we lack the practical tools to get there.

What is improv?

If you have watched a movie or TV show in the last twenty years, I am sure that you have seen someone with improvisational training: Tina Fey, Melissa McCarthy, and Stephen Colbert to name a few. Improv is short for improvisation, which is the act of making something up. Think back to when you were seven and standing in your backyard. No toys, no one telling you what to do. Then you pick up a stick. That stick could become a sword, a guitar, or a magic wand. You were improvising (and you didn't even know it… what a pro!). Kids naturally improvise all of the time. As a teacher, I would wager that you do this no less than 4,353 times per day. We constantly have to think on our feet and come up with new plans on the fly. Copier is jammed? Cool, "Kids, get out your notebook." Half of your class just got called to an assembly? "Alright, plan B. Everyone find a partner and preview the next chapter until they come back." Someone just threw up all over the room including my desk, all of the papers, and three other kids? Ok… well, I guess it can't fix EVERY situation.

If you have never seen *Whose Line is it Anyway* (short form improv) or attended a *Second City* (long form) show, I highly suggest it. Seeing improv being performed is the best way to explain improv. It is magical. The audience and the actors are all in the same environment creating something that has never existed before. Now… that can be a wonderful piece of art or a flaming pile of garbage. And believe me, I have been involved in both, and every situation in between. But the magic is in the moments. The moments of being present. Of creating something. Together.

Rules

Improv only has a few basic rules:

Yes. You accept things that are given to you. If your scene partner says that you are traveling to Mars, that's where you are. If your scene partner says that you are the Queen of England, then... you better start perfecting your wave. This philosophy is not only helpful in improv, but also in teaching. How many times have you planned the perfect lesson to give to the perfect class, except this time, your class got in trouble at recess and half of them are crying when they walked in the door? In this situation, you have two choices. 1. Say "no." Deny the reality. You could plow through with your beautiful lesson plan. Teach over the tears. But how would that turn out? Your objectives would be listed on the board, your boxes would be checked. But did the kids learn anything? I'm betting no. 2. Say "yes." Accept the reality that your students are not in the correct space to learn at the moment. You pivot. Once you accept reality, it is much easier to move forward.

Yes, and. So you have said yes... Now what? In the example above, you might take a minute to do a class circle to talk about it, do some breathing exercises, or do a ten-minute quiet time. Acknowledging the situation is the *yes* and your decisions on where to go from there is the *and*. As teachers, we must accept what our reality is and start making decisions with that information in mind. We can deny reality, or accept it and move on.

Make statements. Have you ever been in this conversation with a friend or partner: "What do you want for dinner?" "I don't know, what do you want for dinner? What sounds good?" "I don't know, what about you?" Is there anything more miserable? These conversations result in nothing but anger. Things happen when we make statements. "I want pizza." "Burgers sound great." Even if the choice is the wrong one, it is better than making no choice at all. I live by this philosophy: I am correct unless someone says, "No Kate, you are wrong." To keep a scene going, we need to make sure that we don't get stuck in a loop of questions by being afraid to make a choice. Asking questions puts your scene partner on the spot and makes them responsible for moving the scene forward. Good things happen when we take responsibility and make bold choices.

Stay in the moment. This one is easier said than done. Teachers are natural multi-taskers. I have also noticed that students are getting better and better at multitasking. At home, they are playing video games, while watching TV, while making videos for YouTube. At school, we are taking attendance, as we collect homework, as we listen to someone explain why they forgot their assignment at home. Improv makes us stay in the present. We have to listen to what is being said, watch what is happening, and think about how we can help move the scene or game forward.

There are no mistakes. When I was first learning improv, one of my teachers told me that the first thing you should think when your scene partner says something is, "That's brilliant!" That simple shift in mindset can open so many doors. We constantly judge things that happen, deciding if it is a *good* or *bad* thing. And in life, yes, there are good and bad things. But in the classroom, sometimes an answer or comment we would never see coming can help us more than any planning ever could. A student can give an incorrect answer and help you realize that you did not explain something clearly enough; a different student might make a connection between a history lesson and a TV show or video game that's popular with the other students. These spontaneous additions can sometimes lead down a path you could have never gotten to if you had rejected them. When we take the approach that whatever is said is brilliant, we allow ourselves to stay in the moment and react. The same is true while playing improv games. We need to allow ourselves to follow paths that we would have not otherwise chosen, because fun lives in spontaneity.

Soft Skills

Our job as educators is to prepare students for their futures. This is usually called "College and Career Readiness". From young students participating in a unit about community helpers to high school students filling out college applications, we always want our students looking to the next step. However, those next steps can be VERY different for each student. Think of an average room full of third graders. Right now, they are all sitting and listening to the same read-aloud or doing the same activity together. Where will all of these students be in 10 years? Some may have joined the military, some may be going into a trade. You may have some children in your class that will be going straight into the workforce or even getting scholarships for Ivy League schools.

With this wide array of options, what practical skills can we teach these students? And what if they change paths? Lots of people do. I definitely cannot address every prerequisite skill that each of these students might need as they navigate the path to their future careers. What I can do is teach them the skills that don't change, the so-called *soft skills*.

What is the difference between a hard skill and a soft skill? Hard skills are skills that you learn and master. Something that you would write on your resume. Proficiency in *Microsoft Word*, conversational Spanish, ability to lift 50 pounds. Now, I don't know about you, but none of those are skills that I am going to be able to teach my kids. Besides that, those skills are fixed. If you are a firefighter, it doesn't matter if you can play the piano (though it would be really cool). Soft skills are transferable skills that can apply to almost any job. These are skills that you can't really study or quantify, but we all know that people are much better off in the workforce if they have them.

Pepperdine University lists the top soft skills as:

- Leadership
- Communication
- Flexibility
- Problem Solving
- Team Building
- Time Management
- Persuasion
- Collaboration
- Seeking Feedback
- Conflict Resolution

Not many curriculums teach these skills, and you cannot really teach them in isolation. Fortunately, improv covers nearly all of them. Let's explore just a few.

Leadership: Anytime you have students leading a game, they must take charge and guide their peers. It can be very intimidating to direct friends or people the same age as you. Learning to keep the game running by simply cutting someone off or sending the attention to someone new makes students pay attention to everyone in the room. It can be empowering when students realize that when they step up and do what needs to be done, everyone wins.

Communication: This is a skill necessary for any job. Students need to learn how to effectively speak and listen to be successful in group work. Improv only works if students both participate in some fashion as well as constantly listen to each other. Speaking is not the only form of communication we use. Body language is an incredibly important and underrated way to communicate feelings. Students must practice identifying and understanding how to read body language.

Flexibility: *Yes, and* is flexibility to a T. Students can have things planned out to the tiniest detail, but if something changes, they need to be willing to change with it. In improv, students never know what will happen next. If they are not flexible, it will not work.

Problem Solving: How many times have you told students, "Go figure it out"? The issue is, problem solving is a skill you develop. A lot of students don't know how to even go about trying to solve problems. If they don't know how to organize that in their heads or plan out the first step, how can we expect them to solve the whole problem? The only way to stretch the muscle of problem solving is by giving students tasks that require them to be creative to overcome challenges. Improv gives the students the safe (and fun) space to stretch that muscle with really nothing on the line if they need help.

Team Building: Not many jobs in life don't require you to work with somebody else in some capacity. Students will have to work for the rest of their lives with groups of other people they may or may not personally like. Again, team building is a skill that cannot be taught from a lecture. Students need to work with others to figure out how to listen to different opinions, share, and celebrate or replan as needed. This can be a challenge for many students (and adults, to be honest). But the earlier students are introduced to team dynamics, the earlier they will learn how to navigate them. Improv can offer that fun way for students to work together to create something. It is amazing to me how quickly improv turns a group into a team. I have done summer camps, half-year clubs, and two-hour workshops. In each of these settings, the students who truly embrace the ideas already have formed a relationship with each other. Improv forces you to take a leap and trust your teammates automatically. When students see that everyone is playing together, they tend to let their guard down and have a little fun. To me, there is no better way of making a connection than laughing with someone.

Linking to Classroom Standards:

Academic Standards

Close your eyes. Imagine yourself in fourth grade. Now, think about math. What is the first thought that comes to your head? Some of you might be cringing at the thought of memorizing multiplication facts or starting to sweat thinking of remembering the steps to long division. I'm thinking of making a birdhouse. We spent a unit studying measurement by creating a birdhouse in class. I remember finding the perimeter and area, using shapes, and ultimately creating a product.

Now, I fully acknowledge that standards from 1997 are different from today's. We cannot do fun, hands-on projects for every lesson. (Have I busted out a worksheet or packet in my time? Oh, for sure.) However, we also know what happens when kids are truly engaged and enjoying a lesson. Their walls break down. They stop judging themselves and start interacting with the material. They laugh. They forget they are learning. That's what an improv-based lesson can provide. Many of these games can be played in ten minutes or less. I am not asking you to throw away your lessons or change your pedagogy. I am suggesting you take a leap to integrate these games into your standards.

Responsive Classroom

According to the *Responsive Classroom* website, there are four main components of the Responsive Classroom approach. These are: Engaging Academics, Positive Community, Effective Management, and Developmentally Responsive Teaching. Improv works with each of these categories.

Engaging Academics: We all know that children learn better when they are engaged in the lesson. When lessons are fun, hands on, and memorable, children enjoy participating more.

Positive Community: We all have been in classrooms that feel like a family and probably have been in ones that feel like strangers sitting next to each other. When students feel safe, loved, and supported in their classroom, they are more likely to be vulnerable and take chances. Growth occurs when we are outside our comfort zone, but it takes preparation to get students there. One of the easiest ways to bond with others is to be silly with them. Sharing a laugh can do so much power in making a connection.

Effective Management: According to *Responsive Classroom*'s website, using effective management "promotes autonomy, responsibility, and high engagement in learning". When students engage in improv, they understand to follow the rules of the game as a participant as well as an audience member. Children learn mutual respect through participating in both of these roles. Children come to see that they don't need to be quiet in the audience because it is a rule, but because they would like the same courtesy from the others when they are playing.

Developmentally Responsive Teaching: We all understand that we cannot treat first graders the same way we treat eighth graders. There are different social and cognitive expectations for each age. Using improv to promote social skills helps students work on skills in confidence, teamwork, communication, as well as many others. The best part of this is that instead of having to find lessons that teach these skills in isolation, these skills are integrated into the games that you are playing.

Social Emotional Skills

Social Emotional skills are something we as teachers have always known are important. Recently, especially after the pandemic, we as a society have started realizing how really important these skills can be. Most social emotional standards fit into three goals and according to the Illinois State Board of Education:

Develop self-awareness and self-management skills to achieve school and life success: Students participating in improv games not only need to pay attention to the people around them, but also must monitor their contributions to the game that is happening. They must learn to read cues from voices, facial expressions, and body language to understand how to proceed. They also must make sure that they are following appropriate rules and boundaries set up in different situations. Students are able to see how their participation in a game led to its success or how they can improve for the future.

Recognize personal qualities and external supports: Most improv games require others to be successful. Students realize while playing these games that relying on others and 'having each other's backs' during these games leads to more positive outcomes. Everyone has different strengths and weaknesses and during improv (and in the classroom). When we focus on the strengths and help each other with areas that need support, we all can succeed.

Demonstrate skills related to achieving personal and academic growth: Unless you have an improv prodigy in your classroom (which you may, and in that case, please call me) students will not start playing these games as rock stars. They will struggle and have to learn how to improve. When students put their minds to giving their best effort, it is amazing how they can use all their skills and come together as a team to achieve that goal.

Speaking and Listening Skills

Common Core Standards are a reality for most teachers in America. While I think that there are many benefits of having standards that every student in America follows, I know that they can be overwhelming. And a lot. Lots of standards, lots of elements to each one of them. How do you fit them all in? As elementary teachers, we know there are the core subjects: ELA, Math, Science, and Social Studies. However, we also have Speaking and Listening standards that we need to cover. Ideally, these should permeate all other classes. And as teachers, we naturally reinforce speaking and listening skills on a daily basis. There are two major objectives for *Speaking and Listening*:

Comprehension and Collaboration: Students learn how to have conversations, work together, and ask for clarification if needed. Improv games require teamwork, turn taking, and communication skills. Students must stay on topic and listen to and follow the rules of the game. They will also need to ask for clarification if they don't understand the rules or elements of a game. During the games, students will collaborate with others to add their ideas and build from there.

Presentation of Knowledge and Ideas: A major part of playing improv games is that there is an audience watching and participating. Children learn how to use their voices, facial expressions, body language, and presence to communicate. Through low-pressure situations and fun, students learn that being in front of others does not have to be scary. They also work on the most important element of public speaking: confidence. Through playing games, children tend to forget about the fear of speaking in front of others. The power of being silly takes down their walls. Once students see that they can be silly, goofy, or do something *incorrectly* in front of a group of people, they can realize that the world will not end if they get embarrassed.

Creating an Improv Culture in Your Classroom

How many times have you been called "Mom"? Daily? Well, at least once a week. Your classroom, be it a self-contained kindergarten class or a middle school math room, is a home away from home. Like at home, we always have classroom rules. Usually these include things like, "Treat others the way you want to be treated," and "Do your best work." Sometimes there are more specific rules: "Hands and feet to yourself," or "Bring all supplies to class." The goal of the rules is to have a class that runs smoothly. There are also consequences when students don't follow the rules. A student may lose points if they forget to bring their homework to class. They may have to write an apology letter if they are unkind to a friend. They may have to sit out of Fun Friday if they don't have all their classwork done.

Rules are important for order. But they usually point out behavior that you don't want, rather than behavior that you do want. We need rules, but we also need guidelines for what students should expect in class. These are not black-and-white rules that someone can measure. These are the ideals that we want our students to think about when they are learning, whether this be with improv or in any other activity.

You are safe: One of the first things I say is 'This classroom is a safe space'. That means that you are safe physically. No one will touch you without your consent. You are also in charge of being safe with your body. This also means that you are safe emotionally. We care about each other and each other's feelings. We don't use words that make each other feel unsafe.

You are free to fail: Whenever I start doing improv in class I say, "Raise your hand if you get paid to perform improv." When no one raises their hand, I say "Well, then none of us are professional improvisers and should not feel pressure to do it correctly. We are all learning every day. And even professionals learn every day." Learning means you are able to do something you were not able to do before. If you can do something perfectly the first time, you already knew how to do it; you didn't need to learn it. Babies fall when they learn to walk. Kids fall when they learn to ride a bike. We will fail when we play improv games. We will fail when we try to spell a word. And we will hold our heads high and move on.

You are brilliant. I tell students to look around the room. Maybe you know everyone by name. Maybe you don't know anyone. I promise you, everyone here is brilliant in their own way. (This could also be a great time to bring up Gardner's Intelligences.) When we work together in improv and in class, I want you to try an experiment. When someone presents an idea, I want the little voice in your head to say, "That's brilliant!" Maybe it wasn't a choice that you would make, but they made it. And it might be the best choice ever.

Assessment Tools

What is a good audience member?

We've all been there, right? You are watching a concert, a movie, or a play. You have turned your cell phone off and are ready to enjoy the show. However, the people next to you decide this is the time to call their grandmother, unwrap every candy in their purse, and sing along. Don't you wish someone would have taught these people how to act as an audience member? I sure do!

Being a good audience member doesn't just apply to performances. Students will have to be on the receiving end of communication, be it to them personally or as a member of a crowd of 500. Students need to understand that their body language, facial expressions, and participation can help or hinder a performance.

What is a good improviser?

If you find a definitive answer to this, please email me. In sports, the team with the most points at the end wins. In theater, music, art, dance, or any other creative field, it is hard to say who is better than whom. In the classroom situation, students are not expected to be experienced actors or orators, they are expected to do their best and communicate as clearly as possible. Unlike in sports, where the end score determines the winner, much of the evaluation of any art form is subjective. We can, however, set certain expectations of students by meeting them where they are. The following rubrics supply structure in elements to look for while students are participating.

Audience Member Rubric

	Attention	Body/Voice	Feedback/Participation	Score
4	Faced stage and players for duration of game Did not engage in any other activity while game was occurring	Body was still during whole performance Voice was only used in appropriate roles	Attempted to offer suggestions when needed Gave audible feedback to players *(laughing/clapping)	
3	Faced stage and players for most of game Engaged in activities that were not distracting to others	Body was mostly still Voice was mostly off during performance	Attempted to offer suggestions when needed OR Gave audible feedback to players *(laughing/clapping)	
2	Faced stage and players for some of the game OR Engaged in other distracting activities	Body was mostly still OR Voice was mostly off	Did not offer any suggestions or audible feedback to players *(laughing/clapping)	
1	Did not face stage Engaged in distracting activities	Student did not have a quiet voice or still body during performance	Gave inappropriate suggestions or feedback	
Total				**___/12**

Performer Rubric

	Voice	Body	Participation	Score
4	Loud speaking voice Allowed others to speak Spoke at a rate that the audience could understand	Safe body Utilized good speaking posture and stage presence during game	Fully committed to the game Gave full effort Supported others in the scene	
3	Speaking voice understandable Allowed others to speak	Safe body Audience was able to see them during the game	Fully committed to the game	
2	Allowed others to speak	Safe body	Attempted the game	
1	Inappropriate use of voice, language, participation	Unsafe body	Inappropriate actions in game or interactions with others	
Total				____/12

The
Games

Job Interview

What ages? This game works best for students in third grade and up.

What classes? This game works well in any class where you want students to experience a different point of view, especially ELA or social studies.

What is the goal? The goal of the game is to have students practice taking on a point of view and answering questions based on that point of view.

How many people play? You can play this game one student at a time or in a panel version where three to four students answer the same questions.

How much time does it take? This is one of the longer games to play, probably five to ten minutes per round. It takes a while to set the character and then get questions from the audience members.

What does the teacher do? The teacher acts as the moderator. They are also usually the one that chooses which job the person is applying for. *The goal is to pick a career that no one would expect the character to do. If you have older students who can handle this, you can also have other students choose.*

What do the other students do? The other students act as audience members and contribute questions that they would ask in an interview. The audience members can also choose to portray a character as they ask questions.

How do you play? The student or students who are playing this game pick or are given a characteristic (gather suggestions from other students: hobbies, characters from a book or period of time). The teacher or other students then pick a job that is unexpected of that character (Example: A student is given the suggestion of a professional wrestler for their character.

The teacher could choose the job of preschool teacher. If you are playing this as a panel game where more than one student is answering questions at a time, either have them all share the same characteristic or choose a job that would be hard for all of them.) The teacher has the characters introduce themselves while the other students think of questions to ask. The teacher acts as the moderator while the audience asks, and the players answer in character. These should be questions that you would see in an interview. The goal is for the person answering to find a way to make their skills transfer to the role for which they are 'applying'. Example, if a professional wrestler got the question 'How will you teach children math?', the answer could be something like "I know that when I pin another wrestler, the guy in the black and white shirt says "1, 2, 3", so I can at least teach up to 3."

How do you debrief? After the game, ask the players what it felt like to answer questions from a different point of view. Did having a strong character make it easier to come up with ideas? Was it hard to answer questions in a way you would not normally answer them?

How can you differentiate?

Students who need scaffolding: This game can be intimidating for students who do not feel confident speaking in front of others or doing improv. Allow students to participate in other ways such as asking questions. If students want to be a player but need guidance, think about giving them a character that they feel very comfortable with (Example: I had a student who loved planes. Anytime he needed to play a character, we gave him that topic and he felt confident enough to participate).

Higher-level students: Give students who need a challenge more detailed characters. Maybe instead of just saying you are a ballerina applying for a construction job, you could add an accent or another adjective (jaded, clumsy).

Link to Academics: *Character traits, Key ideas and details.* Choose a character from a novel you are reading for a student to portray as they interview for a job. Use the information that you have about the characteristics, strengths, weaknesses, and background information to answer these questions. The other students who are asking the questions can also play characters from the novel. Example: The class is reading *Romeo and Juliet.* The student being interviewed is Romeo applying for the job of an apprentice potion maker. The other students who are watching could choose to be themselves or a character like Juliet, Nurse, or Friar Lawrence.

Link to SEL: *Develop self-awareness and self-management skills to achieve school and life success.* Students will be in job interview situations in their lives. Take this opportunity to talk about what is expected in these situations. Make sure you explain that answering in complete sentences, maintaining eye contact, and showing confidence are very important.

Link to Speaking and Listening: *Presentation of knowledge and ideas.* Students will practice asking and answering questions in front of each other. They will need to make sure that they are using the right volume and tone of voice for the situation. Students will have the opportunity to use the power of playing a character to rely on while asking and answering these questions.

This is Your Life

What ages? This game is best for students who are in third grade and above.

What classes? Students can integrate this game into many different academic classes. This game takes a while to play and does not include all students, so it might not be best for morning meetings or during transitions.

What is the goal? The goal is for one student to tell a story and justify pictures while the other students use their bodies to create interesting stage pictures.

How many people play? Each round can have one or two speakers and three to six actors. The actors will not need to speak.

How much time does it take? Since this game has multiple rounds per game (usually three) it takes at least three minutes per round. Since this game has multiple rounds, and each round can take at least three minutes, a typical game of three rounds can last up to ten minutes.

What does the teacher do? The teacher acts as the host. They lead the players in telling the story and guide them on explaining the picture.

What do the other students do? The other students act as good audience members.

How do you play? One or two students are chosen as the speakers. They are given a character or historical figure or can play themselves. The teacher leads them in conversations about the character's life (Usually I do it in chronological order: tell us about your life as a kid, as a young adult, and as an adult. If the child is playing themselves, you could ask about different grades in school). While the speaker is talking to the teacher, the other students behind them are moving around and making different poses. After a few seconds, the teacher yells, "Freeze!" The actors who were posing all must freeze in place. The player or players telling the story then turn around and must justify why this stage picture represents that story that they were just telling. After the justification is over, the players telling the story turn back around and another conversation happens. Each game usually lasts three rounds.

How do you debrief? Ask the students who were playing the silent actors how they were inspired to make certain movements and poses. Did you listen to what the storyteller was talking about previously or did you do the opposite? What was more fun? Ask the storyteller what was the most difficult to justify. Did you find any tricks that could help the next player?

How can you differentiate?

Students who need scaffolding: Students who need help thinking of motions to do behind the speakers can be given a note to mirror what someone else is doing. If a student wants to do the explaining portion but struggles, the teacher can either give them a partner to work with or can ask questions that lead the conversation. The teacher can also give choices. Instead of "What is something else that happened in your life?", the teacher could ask, "Do you want to talk about school or your hobbies?"

Higher-level students: Higher-level students can host the game, asking questions to the speaker.

Link to Academics: *ELA-Literature: Key ideas and details: Character studies, summarizing.* This is a great activity for students to practice summarizing a story. You could ask the students what happened at the beginning, middle, and end of a story you read, and they would have to justify what the picture is showing about their statements.

Link to SEL: *Use social-awareness and interpersonal skills to establish and maintain positive relationships.* Part of being aware of what is happening around you socially is reading body language. The storytellers must read what the actors are portraying with no words. The actors must use social awareness to make sure they are working together to give a good stage picture. They also can use facial expressions and body postures to show emotions.

Link to Speaking and Listening: *Comprehension and collaboration, presentation of knowledge and ideas.* The speaker in this game must tell a story with confidence. They must listen to the questions being asked and give coherent answers made up on the spot.

Snowball Toss

What ages? This game can be played with any age.

What classes? This game is short, so it can be played during brain breaks, morning meetings, closing circle, or any other time a break is needed.

What is the goal? The goal for this game is to practice pantomime in action and reaction. This also requires students to practice *Yes, and.*

How many people play? This game can be played with any size group. If you have a group larger than 15, I would suggest breaking into smaller groups once the students know how to play. This way, children will get more chances to participate.

How much time does it take? This game is meant to take a short amount of time, and you can probably get through a whole class in around five minutes. If you would like to extend the time, you can add different rules each round.

What does the teacher do? The teacher introduces the game and then observes and makes comments when needed. If this game is being played with a large group, the teacher can encourage students to make sure they are including all children and help everyone know who has not gotten a turn.

What do the other students do? All students play this game at the same time. Even though they might not be actively participating, they will have to focus and pay attention because they never know when it will be their turn.

How do you play? The teacher will tell the students that they will be having an indoor snowball fight. You need to find a way to show how big the snowball is. (How much snow did you use? How heavy is it?) Then, you decide on a person to throw it to. You need to decide how to throw it: Roll it? Baseball pitch? Toss? The person who you are throwing it to will need to react to the throw and the size of the snowball. Once they have reacted, it is their turn to make a snowball and throw it. Play until everyone has had a turn or until time is up.

How do you debrief?

How did you show details about your snowball? How did you use your body and your face? How did others' actions affect the way that you reacted?

How can you differentiate?

Students who need scaffolding: Most students can play this game with little or no help. If students are stuck, verbally tell them step by step what to do, "First, make a snowball. Now, who do you want to throw it to?"

Higher-level students: Students can be given specific ways to throw the snowball.

Link to Academics: *Learning parts of speech (adjectives and adverbs)*. This game can easily be integrated into teaching adverbs. Students can be given different adverbs on how to throw the snowball. (lightly, quickly...). You could also use adjectives to describe the snowball (Throw a snowball that is hard, that is humungous, that is freezing).

Link to SEL: *Use social-awareness and interpersonal skills to establish and maintain positive relationships.* Students need to use verbal cues and eye contact to communicate with each other. They also need to read and react to others' body language.

Link to Speaking and Listening: *Presentation of knowledge and ideas.* Part of listening and speaking is using nonverbal cues, such as reading body language and paying attention to eye contact. Through this exercise, students must rely on communicating through these modes.

Late for School

What ages? This game can be played with students third grade and up. The higher the grade, the more challenging you can make the rule.

What classes? This game is great for transition times but also is fun when talking about genres.

What is the goal? The goal of this game is for students to follow a rule given by the teacher and come up with a reason that they are late for school.

How many people play? This game is played one person at a time. The students take turns playing and anyone who wants to be involved can play.

How much time does it take? This game can have a set amount of time and you can end it when you need to. It could take less than five minutes.

What does the teacher do? The teacher sets up a rule for the students to follow. They also are the one that chooses which children can give their excuses.

What do the other students do? The other students wait their turn or think of new rules to use.

How do you play? The teacher (or other students in older grades) set a rule. Once the rule is set, students try to give an excuse for why they are late to school following that rule. Example: The rule is you must use alliteration in your sentence. Student: Sorry I'm late Mrs. W, my mom made me move a mile before school! My sister sat on my squirrel Sam! You have to use seven words: Student: I was out all night picking flowers. Students also need to sell their excuses to make the teacher believe it (big facial expressions, tone of voice, movements).

How do you debrief? Ask the students what their game plan was. Did they sit and think out their whole excuse first? Did they just open their mouths and hope something would come out?

How can you differentiate?

Students who need scaffolding: This game can be hard because it is fast-paced. Try to do one round that doesn't have to do with the words (make up an excuse a bear would say, sing your excuse, etc.). For children who need more time, you can provide the categories before the game begins. This is a game that some students may not want to join in for, and that is ok. If there are students who want to participate but are having a hard time, they can also play the teacher accepting excuses. This way, they can just say whether they would take the excuse or not.

Higher-level students: Challenge students who can handle it with wordplay. Introduce new literary terms before you play: assonance, prose, onomatopoeia.

Link to Academics: *ELA: Vocabulary acquisition and use: Figurative language.* Word relationships, and nuances. Poetry and figurative language seems to be a standard that can be difficult to get to in the sequence of our teaching. Using games like this can introduce and integrate these skills into small games. Besides just alliteration, you could have students use a different literary device: rhyming, metaphors, onomatopoeia.

Link to SEL: *Develop self-awareness and self-management skills to achieve school and life success.* This game allows students to use different emotions. Challenge students to use their voice, gestures, and body language to show emotion while giving an excuse. What is different in someone's voice if they are mad compared to scared? What is the difference between body language in someone bored and tired?

Link to Speaking and Listening: *Presentation of knowledge and ideas.* This game is meant to be performed in front of others, but there is only one line to say. Students need to make sure they are speaking clearly and loudly enough for others to hear.

In a World...

What ages? This game is best played with grades five and up. Younger students can also do this with more guidance.

What classes? This game is great for brainstorming ideas for writing, but can also be used in other ways.

What is the goal? The goal is for the student to come up with a movie pitch when given three items. They also must give us the title of the movie. They will always start the pitch with the line "In a world..." and sell this movie using an announcer voice like they are watching a preview.

How many people play? This game is played by the whole class. Students make the pitch one person at a time, but the other students are thinking of suggestions or waiting their turn during the pitches.

How much time does it take? This game can take as long or as short as the teacher wants. It can be played so all students get a turn, or just for a few rounds.

What does the teacher do? The teacher directs the flow of the game and whose turn it is. They also put together suggestions for the player.

What do the other students do? The other students give suggestions and act as audience members.

How do you play? Students give suggestions of nouns. This can either be on a piece of paper, written on a white board, or during each round (the easiest is to get all of the suggestions before the game starts). One student at a time is called on to be the producer. They are given three items and must come up with a movie idea including the objects. Example: A truck, grapes, and an amusement park. Student: (in an announcer's voice): In a world where there is a family that just wants to visit an amusement park. They decide to grow some grapes to win the state fair and earn enough money to fix up their truck to drive to the amusement park for vacation. This summer we present "Roller Coasters are GRAPE".

How do you debrief? Ask students what they did to incorporate all the ideas. Did you have any ideas before you got up? Did you make any connections to the items; were those easier to incorporate?

How can you differentiate?

Students who need scaffolding: Students who have a difficult time can be put with a buddy or given fewer suggestions. Example: Give me a movie about an orange. You can also have students work as a team.

Higher-level students: Challenge your higher-level students with more challenging vocabulary. You can also give them more than three items.

Link to Academics: *ELA: Writing narratives.* You can play this game with students and then give them 5-10 minutes to write a short story. Students could do this short write on their own or with another student.

Link to SEL: *Develop self-awareness and self-management skills to achieve school and life success.* Sometimes in life, you don't get what you expected. While playing this game, explain to students that sometimes you just have to use the ingredients that you are given to make something work.

Link to Speaking and Listening: *Presentation of knowledge and ideas.* This game is all about self-confidence and convincing people that you have a great idea. I always tell my kids that if you pretend you know what you are doing, people will believe you. Tell children to lean into the character of the confident producer and see how it feels to pretend you know what you're doing.

Kitty Cat Vocab

What ages? Kids in third grade and up can play this game.

What classes? This game is great for any class that has vocabulary: ELA, science, social studies, and more.

What is the goal? Players will act out vocabulary words for the other students to guess. The trick is, the players must act out the clue like a cat would act it out. They are allowed to only make cat sounds and pantomime to get others to guess the word.

How many people play? One person acts out clues at a time. The other students are watching and preparing to guess.

How much time does it take? This game can be played one time or as many times as you would like. It usually takes less than two minutes per round. If you have a list of specific words to choose from, it usually takes less time.

What does the teacher do? The teacher chooses which child will be acting, facilitates the guessing, and helps students choose topics or words to act out.

What do the other students do? The other students act as audience members and raise their hand to guess what the actor is acting out.

How do you play? Students are given a list of vocabulary words. One student is chosen to act out one of the words, only using sounds and movements that a cat would use. Audience members raise their hand when they think they know the answer and the teacher calls on them one at a time. Once someone guesses correctly, he gets a turn at acting out a word. Game continues for the length of time you have or until everyone has had a chance to go.

How do you debrief? Ask the students what some of the biggest clues were while they were guessing. What is an example of a really good clue? As an actor, how did you choose what to do? Did meowing and making noise help? How?

How can you differentiate?

Students who need scaffolding: If students are not sure where to start, whisper or write a word that they know, so they do not have to choose amongst all of the words. They also can bring a buddy with them if needed.

Higher-level students: If students are comfortable in this game, you can allow them to choose different animals. (We had a student invent Kangaroo Charades where you have to act out something while jumping the whole time – Thanks Amari!)

Link to Academics: *ELA: Vocabulary acquisition and use.* We all know that memorizing vocabulary words on flashcards or through rote memorization does not work with everyone. Using different modalities can help children remember what words mean.

Link to SEL: *Develop self-awareness and self-management skills to achieve school and life success.* This game requires confidence in performing something silly in front of peers. While one student is acting, all of the other students are supporting them by guessing. The whole class is laughing together which builds community.

Link to Speaking and Listening: *Presentation of knowledge and ideas.* This game takes away language so students are forced to rely on body language. Players need to find a clear way to demonstrate something and the audience needs to pay attention to just body language.

Emoji or Throwing Faces

(Thank you to Stephanie for the name)

What ages? This game can be played with any age.

What classes? Since this is a short game that focuses on SEL standards, it is perfect for morning meetings, closing circles, or transitions.

What is the goal? The goal is to demonstrate different emotions.

How many people play? The whole class is engaged in this game. Groups of four to twenty can play.

How much time does it take? Each person's turn should take less than 20 seconds, even if they need assistance, so it can all be done in around five minutes.

What does the teacher do? The teacher starts the game and then steps in as needed. This might require being ready to scaffold and provide examples as needed.

What do the other students do? The other students watch the game and wait for their turn. Students never know when their turn will occur, so they must stay engaged the whole time.

How do you play? The students gather in a circle. The teacher starts off showing an emotion on their face. Then they pretend to put it in their hand, say someone's name, and *throw* it at the person. That person *catches* the emotion and then puts it on their face. They then turn around and display another emotion. They turn back around and repeat the process until everyone has had a chance to go.

How do you debrief? Ask students how they can demonstrate different emotions. Is it just your face, or also your body? Which emotions are harder to demonstrate or identify? This is also a great time to explain that not everyone is good at showing or interpreting facial expressions. Playing this game can help students to better understand facial expressions, emotions, and body language.

How can you differentiate?

Students who need scaffolding: Provide a list of emotions beforehand so students can reference them if they don't know what to do. Give a few examples before you start as well. If students are totally stuck, they can repeat one of your examples.

Higher-level students: Challenge higher-level students to think of degrees of emotion. How can you show the difference between disappointed and furious, between melancholy and devastated? Challenge these children to incorporate their whole body to show each emotion.

Link to Academics: *Demonstrate command of the conventions of standard English grammar and usage when writing or speaking.* The teacher could change the game to throwing verbs. (Someone is running then throws that to someone else. That person runs and then morphs it into another motion.)

Link to SEL: *Use social-awareness and interpersonal skills to establish and maintain positive relationships.* After this game, go around and talk about the emotions that different people showed. Ask how they decided to demonstrate that emotion. Could people do it in different ways? What else shows a certain emotion? How can you identify emotions in people?

Link to Speaking and Listening: *Presentation of knowledge and idea.* After this game, talk about how important facial expressions are and what we can communicate through just our face.

Commercial

What ages? This game can be played with grades three and up.

What classes? It is great for breaks and can also be integrated into academic areas.

What is the goal? The goal of the game is to develop a character. The students will use this character to develop a short 10-15 second commercial of a product.

How many people play? This game has one person playing at a time. However, once students understand how to play the game, they can be separated into smaller groups to play.

How much time does it take? Each round takes less than a minute. You can play as many rounds as you want per game.

What does the teacher do? The teacher acts as the host of the show. She also is the one assigning characters to the students.

What do the other students do? The other students act as good audience members.

How do you play? Students are instructed to find an object. This can be from their desk, from the classroom, or they can draw an item quickly on a piece of paper. The teacher selects a student. Next, the teacher assigns the student a character. This can be through pulling characters out of a hat, rolling dice that represent characters, or using a character wheel (example:

https://wordwall.net/resource/392377/character-wheel). The student has 10-15 seconds to sell their item as the character. Play continues with another student and another character. Example: You are selling a stapler as a superhero!

How do you debrief? Ask students what they did to get into character. Ask the audience what they noticed about the performance. What was changed: facial expressions, voice, word choice? How did the students use their point of view in their commercials?

How can you differentiate?

Students who need scaffolding: If students cannot do a commercial on their own, treat it more like an interview. Have them answer the questions as the character. Some examples: What is your product? What does it do? Why should people buy it? Encourage the students that whatever they think the character sounds like is the correct choice.

Higher-level students: If students are successful in this game and require a challenge, tell them that they have to sell the item that they chose, but they cannot use it for the purpose that it is intended. Example: If they chose a pencil, they cannot use it to write. They could, however, say it is a great fake mustache when you need a disguise or can be used to play a one-handed drum set.

Link to Academics: *Character studies, point of view.* This game is about characters and point of view and can be integrated into lessons during ELA instruction. This game can also be put into other content areas. If you are learning about different types of rocks or elements in science, have the students do a commercial telling you everything they know about it. If you are learning about different forms of government, have students give brief commercials about the pros of each kind. This game can also be integrated into special areas in PE, Media, Music, and Art. Students can give commercials of different musical instruments, sports, books, or artists. The nice thing about this game also is there are no right or wrong answers. Children with basic knowledge of a topic can share that, students with higher-level content knowledge can use that.

Link to SEL: *Develop self-awareness and self-management skills to achieve school and life success.* Giving students a character to focus on allows them to get out of their head and open up more than asking them to speak as themselves. Students are allowed to be wrong and silly because it is not them speaking, it is the character. Developing the confidence to speak in front of others is sometimes a large barrier for students. However, once students see that they can do it and others think they did a good job, they are more likely to want to participate more.

Link to Speaking and Listening: *Presentation of knowledge and ideas.* Presenting ideas is a large part of many careers as well as many classes in high school and college. During this game, students will have to speak confidently as they are thinking on their feet. Talk about what kind of tone of voice and body language you need to use while presenting in front of others.

*This is a game that is only played one student at a time. Because of this, it can be very short. You could play this game during a transition, for a brain break, or a small group could play this game as an independent activity.

Instruction Manual

What ages? This game can be played with fifth graders and up. Younger children will need more coaching.

What classes? Content areas work well for this game, like science and social studies.

What is the goal? The goal is to work as a team to explain parts of an instruction manual on a given topic. Students will need to listen to each other and pick up right where the last person ended their sentence.

How many people play? This game works best with between 3-6 players at a time. You can play multiple rounds in the same sitting.

How much time does it take? The teacher gets to control the pacing and timing of this game, so it can take as much or as little time as you would like. Minimum, it would probably be around 3-4 minutes per round.

What does the teacher do? The teacher conducts this game by either pointing to a new player, saying a new player's name, or both.

What do the other students do? The other students act as the audience. They will also be called upon to give additional chapters in the instructional manual.

How do you play? A group of 4-6 players is called up to the front of the room. The teacher gets a topic or object that would have an instructional manual (Scooter, Air fryer). The teacher starts conducting the students to tell the introduction of the instruction manual. The teacher points to a student, who begins speaking as though reading the instruction manual for the given object. At any point, the teacher points to a different student who must continue the manual. The teacher can stop after a sentence, during a sentence, or even in the middle of a word. Once the teacher feels like the chapter is done, they ask the audience for a new part of the instruction manual (FAQs, cleaning the product, the history of the product). Depending on the age of the students, the teacher might have to scaffold to get chapter titles.

How do you debrief?

Ask students what skills they need to play this game well. How did listening help? What can you do if you don't know what to say?

How can you differentiate?

Students who need scaffolding: For students who struggle keeping up with the pace, make sure they only are only given the story during a natural break, like at the end of the sentence. Also, make sure they have warning that their turn is coming. If a student is still stuck, repeat some of the information the last student gave and ask the student a question. For example, "Grace just said that you need to clean the microwave once a week. How would you clean it?". If the student is still hesitant, the teacher asks a yes or no question and restates the information they added. Teacher points to Seth. Seth doesn't know what to say. Teacher: "Seth, Mary just said you need to wear shoes when you ride the scooter. Do you need to wear anything else?" Seth says nothing. Teacher: "Do you think they need a helmet?". Seth nods. Teacher: "Perfect, so Seth said you also need to wear a helmet when you ride the scooter."

Higher-level students: Teachers can make this game more difficult by moving from child to child more quickly or at a random pace. Once audience members give suggestions for chapters, the teacher can add additional layers on top of it like, "You must do this chapter in gibberish, as a 90 year old, or as someone who is really confused."

Link to Academics: *Summarizing, content review.* This game can be a great review before a test. The students can discuss what they know about the unit they were studying. Example: If the students are going to take a quiz over a novel they read, the first instruction manual could be characters in the book. They could get a different character each time and tell everything they know about those characters. This also would be a great game to play in a hands-on class like art or cooking. Students would have to give different steps in using clay or baking a pie.

Link to SEL: *Use social-awareness and interpersonal skills to establish and maintain positive relationships.* Teachers could use the same strategies in applying this game to SEL situations. Instead of doing chapters in the instructional manual, teachers could get different situations from the audience members. The theme could be "kindness" and the teacher could ask for different situations where it might be hard to be kind. Or the teacher could talk about conflict resolution and the students could get different scenarios and have to give instructions on how to navigate that situation.

Link to Speaking and Listening: *Presentation of knowledge and ideas.* Since students will be working together in this game, they will have to listen very carefully so they can continue the train of thought. Talk about active listening. How can you position your body to make sure you are listening to the person speaking?

Uber

What ages? I have played this game with students grades three and up. The higher the grade, the deeper into characters you can get.

What classes? This class is a fun break or reward activity. It can also work well with ELA or in any subject where students are learning about specific characters.

What is the goal? The goal of this game is to develop characters. The bonus of this game is that not only does one person start the character, but the other player must mirror the character, taking on the voice, facial expressions, and body language of the other actor.

How many people play? Usually, this game is played with all players standing in line. The first person to be the driver goes to the end of the line and becomes the last player entering. I have played with up to 14-15 kids at a time (be aware, the more kids you have, the longer it takes). You can also do it with as small of a group as three (keep having kids come back in as different characters each time).

How much time does it take? This game usually needs at least thirty seconds per pair. So, depending on how many people you have, it might take a while.

What does the teacher do? The teacher initiates the Uber driver to leave with some signal (bell, chime, clap). They must also side-coach if needed to help the scene keep going. The teacher should start looking for an out of a scene (usually a funny part) after about thirty seconds. Don't let the scene go on longer than a minute. Depending on the age of the students, give them suggestions of how to be inspired to come in. Usually with younger students who don't have much acting experience, I encourage them to just choose to come in with an emotion (or have emotion cards read to hand them). Older students can use more body movements and accents.

What do the other students do? This game can be played with very short scenes, so other students who are watching will probably have a turn. Students can write down descriptions of each round for the discussion after. They also should be paying attention to try and make different choices of characters than others have made.

How do you play? Two chairs are put in the front of the room. Students who are playing line up on the side of the classroom. The teacher quickly discusses what we use to act (facial expressions, voice, body language). One student is selected to be the first Uber driver. They sit down and pretend to start driving. Another student enters from the line of players and sits down in the passenger seat. They initiate a character to the driver (Example: If they are mad, they slam the door, exhale loudly, and say something about how they are having a bad day). The Uber driver must immediately *Yes, and* that character trait and interact with the other player, mirroring their character (important to note, they are not mirroring the words, just the characteristics.) The scene goes on until the teacher gives the signal to end the scene. The actor playing the driver says something like "Well my shift is over," and leaves the scene. The actor who was playing the passenger moves over and is now the driver. The scene proceeds with a new passenger. Continue this pattern until the actor who was the first driver gets to be the passenger.

How do you debrief? Ask the students how they initiated a character. Were they inspired by a character that already exists? Did they choose an emotion?

How can you differentiate?

Students who need scaffolding: For students who have less experience, write a list of emotions or characteristics on the board. Do a few examples of how you can show these through your voice, face, and body. If a student gets stuck, help them choose an emotion on the board. You can also purchase emotion cards that have the word and a visual to assist students who need more support.

Higher-level students: Encourage students to use a different voice to be or an age that they are not. You can also encourage students who are more advanced to build longer, more detailed scenes. Object work is another thing that can be built in. If a student picks being a high-power business person with a phone and a laptop, show us both in the car!

Link to Academics: *Character traits.* This game can be used while introducing character traits. Have a bowl of character traits that students can pull from when they go into the scene. After the driver mirrors them, they guess what the characteristic was. You can also choose to act as characters from books, people from a history unit, or even organs of the body. Use your imagination to choose how students could embody different ideas!

Link to SEL: *Use social-awareness and interpersonal skills to establish and maintain positive relationships.* Instead of mirroring an emotion, have the driver try to balance the person who comes in. If the person is mad or sad, have the driver help calm them down or solve the problem. If the person is really happy, be serious.

Link to Speaking and Listening: *Presentation of knowledge and ideas.* These scenes are all conversations between two people. Talk about how to take turns and not speak over each other.

*This game is best played with groups of students who have some understanding of character and scene work.

Yay-Boo

What ages? This game can be played with grades three and up. The lower the grade, the less connected the statements need to be. For older students, encourage the statements to connect to a story.

What classes? This game can be played in academic classes as well as homeroom, morning meeting, or advisory.

What is the goal? The goal of this game is to work on active listening and adding on to a story. This is also a good game to tell the difference between *yes* and *no* in an improv game. We can make situations worse (no) while still accepting an offer (yes) someone has given us. This also teaches children how to stay in the moment, since they cannot decide what they are going to say until they hear the statement right before they speak.

How many people play? This game can be played with 3 players and up. If you have fewer students, they will get to have more than one turn. If you have over twenty students, everyone will only get to add one sentence.

How much time does it take? This game can either go until everyone gets a turn or a set time. Usually, it will finish in about five minutes.

What does the teacher do? The teacher acts as the conductor of the story. They will get the title and make sure the students know the order. Depending on the age of the students, the teacher may also have to make sure that the story stays on topic. They may also add information and jump ahead in the story. (For example, if the students are stuck talking about a character for a few rounds, the teacher could say, "Ok, now in chapter 3 in this book, Emily decided to go on an adventure.") Usually, this will get the students out of the rut and allow them to explore more ideas.

What do the other students do? The great thing about this game is the students are actively engaged the whole time! After each statement is added to the story, the other students either yell "Yay!" or "Boo!". The students also need to be actively listening so when their turn comes up, they know what to add. The other students also need to act like a good audience when it is not their turn.

How do you play? The goal of the game is to tell a story that has never been told before one sentence at a time. However, the pattern of the story goes: good statement, bad statement. After each good statement, the rest of the students say "Yay!". After each bad statement, the rest of the class says "Boo!". If the story was called The Little Lobster, the story could go like this: 1. Once upon a time, there was a lobster named Marvin. (Rest of the kids – Yay!). 2. He was sad because he was a lot smaller than the other lobsters. (Rest of the kids – Boo!) 3. But, he had lots of friends! (Rest of the kids – Yay!) 4. Until one day, his parents told him they would have to move to another ocean. (Rest of the kids – Boo!) This can go on as long as you want the story to last or until everyone has had a chance to go at least once.

How do you debrief? Ask the students what they needed to do to play this game well. Make sure you talk about active listening. Talk about which one was more fun and why. See if anyone can summarize the story in a few sentences. Talk about how adding good and bad things heighten the story.

How can you differentiate?

Students who need scaffolding: When students first play this game, don't worry as much about them keeping a story structure. If there are only certain students who are struggling, have them add details to the last sentence rather than move the story ahead. Example: Student A – "There once was a girl named Sue." (YAY!) Student B – "She was sad because she lost her teddy bear." (Boo!) Student C – gets stuck. Teacher – "What color is the teddy bear?" Student C – "Blue." Teacher – "Say, 'the teddy bear was blue.'" Student C – "The teddy bear was blue." (YAY!) The bigger goal for some students is to be included rather than adding information.

Higher-level students: Higher-level students need to be encouraged to stay on topic. They also can be encouraged to add dialogue to their statements. Encourage higher-level students to also act out their statement with the emotion that they are portraying.

Link to Academics: *Key ideas and details.* This story can be played to talk about story structure. You can take out the "Yay! Boo!" portion of it and just do Story Sentence at a Time if needed. That game is played by just adding one sentence at a time to complete a story. You can have a chart on the board about what you need at the beginning, middle and end of the story. Stop frequently and show where you are on the chart. When teaching about summaries, you could also play this game first and then practice summarizing on the board.

Link to SEL: *Develop self-management skills.* This is a good game to get kids out of their heads. If you have students that are hesitant to play, you can make sure they know that you will coach them. Each statement that is said is met with a Yay! or Boo! and is part of making the story complete.

Link to Speaking and Listening: *Presentation of knowledge and ideas.* Talk to students about how your voice changes between good news and bad news. What happens to the tone, speech, and volume of your voice?

*This activity is good for students who have some concept of story structure. Students should also be able to understand that bad doesn't mean violent or depressing. I would make sure that students have done some improv games before this one.

Dr. Know It All

What ages? Students in third grade and up can play this game.

What classes? This game is great for any classes during a unit review or when introducing new concepts. It is also a fun game to play during morning meetings.

What is the goal? The goal of this game is for all of the students to speak as one person. Each student playing represents one head of the smartest person alive, Dr. Know It All. The audience gives Dr. Know It All questions that start with "how" or "why" like, "Why is the sky blue?" and "How do I make a Thanksgiving feast?". The students answer the question one word at a time.

How many people play? Dr. Know It All is best played with between three and six students. Four is usually the ideal, but it can be modified to best suit your class. You can also play multiple rounds of this game so all students can have a turn.

How much time does it take? The teacher leads the game by getting suggestions of questions, so they really can end the game after any question they want. Each answer should take around a minute to give.

What does the teacher do? The teacher acts as the host for this game. She introduces Dr. Know It All and give a practice question, usually, "How are you today?". Encourage students to answer questions in full sentences. The teacher also gets questions from the audience, modifying them if needed. When I play this game, I usually move the start of the answer down the row of heads. So, if the first person starts the first answer, I would have the second person start the second answer. This breaks up the pattern of the answers and makes the students pay attention more.

What do the other students do? The other students act as the audience members during this game. They also come up with questions for Dr. Know It All to answer. These questions should be open ended questions; usually ones that start with "how" or "why" tend to work best.

How do you play? Students stand in front of the audience in a line. The teacher gives them a practice question like, "How are you today, Dr. Know It All?". She then tells the students which head will begin, and the students answer that question one word at a time. When the students have finished, she cues them to take a bow. After this, the teacher asks for questions from the audience. The teacher restates the questions to Dr. Know It All and tells them which head will start the answer. When any student playing feels the answer is finished, they will say 'period'. They will initiate a bow and the others will follow to show the end of the answer. The teacher can also add in the word 'Period' to end a round if it is going on too long. Continue this pattern for as many questions per round as you want. Multiple rounds can be played to let all students have a turn. Tell students that they do not have to answer the question with any specific answer, but their sentence needs to make sense grammatically.

How do you debrief? This game depends on being able to listen to each other. Talk to students about why it is important to listen to each other. Even though there are no wrong answers, how can we make a better answer that makes more sense? Ask if there were any times that students weren't sure what to say. How did they figure out how to keep moving forward with the answer? Did any students have trouble hearing what was said? How can we make that better in the next round?

How can you differentiate?

Students who need scaffolding: Put students who might need more help closer to the end of the line so they have time to see how the other children are playing the game. If a student gets stuck, repeat the sentence for them to hear again, prompting them to add one word. If they are still stuck, try to give them two options. Example: The sky is blue because… (Student does not answer.) Teacher: "Ok, the sentence was, 'The sky is blue because…'" (Student still does not answer.) "Would you say 'if' or 'before'?" Student: "if." Teacher repeats the whole sentence with that word and the game continues. I have played this game with students with varying abilities and ages, and most students pick up on it. If there is a student who either does not want to play or is not able to participate, you can have them be your assistant host and they can choose students in the audience to ask questions.

Higher-level students: If students understand this game, you can start allowing them to host it instead of you. Students can also add characters on top of their answers. They are playing the smartest person in the world, so encourage them to use *smart* voices and gestures as they play.

Link to Academics: *Restating question, writing complete sentences.* This is one of my favorite games to teach students how to restate a question. In many types of testing, students must answer questions in complete sentences, restating the question. Before you play this game, review the steps of how to restate a question. Example: If the question is, "Why is the sky blue?", you would start the answer with, "The sky is blue because…"

Link to SEL: *Use social-awareness and interpersonal skills to maintain positive relationships.* This whole game is based on working together. Students need to make sure to pay attention to those around them and listen to what they are saying. Students will also usually realize what players may need more time, the word repeated, or other assistance. Encourage students to support their fellow players in any way they can.

Link to Speaking and Listening: *Comprehension and collaboration.* Since students are only allowed to add one word at a time, they must actively listen during this game. They also need to make sure that they are speaking loud enough to be heard by not only the audience but all players.

*This game is best used once students have some familiarity with each other. They also should have some knowledge of *Yes, and.*

Try That On For Size

What ages? This game can be played with students grades three and up as a competition. Younger students can play this game with modifications listed in the differentiated portion.

What classes? This is a fun game for a transition time. Students may also play during morning meetings or closing circles. This game is pretty physical so it is also a good choice for a brain break.

What is the goal? The goal of this game is to brainstorm different ideas for the same movement. Students must be creative and think of different reasons they would be doing a motion. The other important part of this game is having students saying what they are doing with confidence, even if they feel silly or wrong.

How many people play? This game can be played in two ways. In one way, students are lined up in front of the room. The action moves down the line and repeats until a student is eliminated. In this scenario, the line should include four to six students. Another way to play this is head-to-head, which involves two students at a time. In a classroom setting, I would usually choose the first option. You can play this game with multiple rounds to include all students.

How much time does it take? This game is determined by how long it takes for students to get eliminated.

What does the teacher do? The teacher gets the suggestions from the audience to give to the players. While the students are playing, the teacher also needs to end the rounds. They can either do this by eliminating a person because they either didn't have something to say, they repeated an action, or what they did didn't make sense. If you do not want to play it elimination style, the teacher can end the round whenever they want.

What do the other students do? The other students act as the audience during this game. They also give suggestions whenever it is needed.

How do you play?

Line game style: Between four and six students go to the front of the room. The teacher gets suggestions for an action (painting a wall, shooting a basketball). The first student in line does the action and says what he or she is doing ("I am shooting a basketball, try that on for size"). The next student in line does the same action and gives another reason for why you would be doing that action ("I am petting an elephant, try that on for size"). The action continues down the line with students giving other reasons for doing the same motion. The teacher stops the round when someone can't think of something, someone repeats, or the teacher doesn't think the explanation makes sense (this will vary a lot depending on age). Once someone is out, another suggestion is given, and play continues with the person that would have gone after the student that was kicked out. Play continues until time is up or one person is left.

One on one: In this version of the game, only two children play in a head-to-head style. They must quickly go back and forth until one is eliminated. The person who won gets to stay in for another round and another player goes in for the eliminated player. When this game is performed on stage, this is usually how it is played. However, fewer people get to play at a time.

How do you debrief? Ask the students how they thought up new ideas. What is the difference between a right and a wrong idea? How does confidence play into this game? How do you think you could carry that into your life?

How can you differentiate?

Students who need scaffolding: Some students have a difficult time losing. In this game, talk about how losing is actually good because it means more people get to play. If there is someone having a hard time with this, make sure they get high fives and are told we are now counting on them as the cheering section.

Higher-level students: The teacher controls how easy or hard this game is. If you have students that are good at it, call it tougher. Give them less time to think between players, call them out if their action doesn't make much sense or if you just don't like it (they will think it's funny... I promise) or make them sit down if they do not deliver with more confidence. You might end up judging students differently at this game, but as educators, we know that we must differentiate for our students' strengths.

Link to Academics: *Content specific goals.* This game could be integrated into PE. Start with an activity from a sport (shooting a basket, serving a volleyball). Have students then think of other ways they can use that movement in other sports or physical activities.

Link to SEL: *Develop self-management skills.* Students will need to think on their feet and be confident during this game. When I play it, I tell kids, "If you sell it, I will usually buy it." This means that even if your activity doesn't totally make sense, and you say it with confidence, I will probably not call you out. Talk about why it is so important to speak with a confident voice.

Link to Speaking and Listening: *Presentation of knowledge.* This is a performance game, so explain to children that they need to speak clearly and loudly enough for all players and audience members to hear.

*This game is a good introductory activity to play. It does not rely on communication between students and there are no characters involved. Students need some knowledge of using confidence and *Yes, and.*

Categories

What ages? This game is appropriate for all grades, depending on the level of difficulty.

What classes? This is a good game to play in transitions or SEL times, but it also can be integrated into almost any academic class.

What is the goal? The goal of this game is to think quickly on your feet. Students will also need to listen to each other and take turns.

How many people play? To play this as an elimination game, groups of four to seven are best. If playing this way, the rest of the students act as the audience members, ready to give new suggestions when needed. If you are not playing as an elimination game, you can have all students play at the same time and raise their hand when they have something to add.

How much time does it take? When playing this game as an elimination game, you continue until there is one student left. Give yourself at least five minutes per round. If you want to play this game with the whole group, you can just end the game whenever you want. (Be aware, with younger students, they will usually all want a turn. In this case, I would also leave at least 5 minutes.)

What does the teacher do? The teacher gets suggestions of categories from the audience. The broader the category, the easier. The teacher also chooses which student goes next, either by calling students randomly in the elimination way to play or by calling people who have their hand up in the whole group play.

What do the other students do? Students who are not playing act as good audience members and think of new categories for future rounds.

How do you play?

Elimination style play: Between four to seven students stand in the front of the room. The teacher gets a category from the audience. (If the category is too specific, it is the teacher's job to make it more broad). The teacher calls a student's name or points at a student, and he or she names something that fits in that category (colors, shapes, states). The teacher keeps calling on students to name things in that category. If the student hesitates for too long, repeats, can't think of anything, or says something that doesn't fit in the category, they are eliminated. (Sometimes it is hard for kids to lose in front of others. If this is the case, tell them when they get eliminated, they get to stage a performance back to their seat where they must act like they are devastated, including fake crying and pouting. That way, if they actually are upset, no one will know). Play continues until one student is declared the winner.

Whole group play: In this version, have all of the students who want to play stand up. The teacher gets a category (preferably from a student who doesn't want to play). Students raise their hand if they have something to fit in the category. Once they have participated, they sit back down. Play goes until everyone is sitting.

How do you debrief? Talk to students about thinking on their feet. What strategies did you use to think of things to say? If you are playing the elimination round, talk about how it feels to lose. What would happen if no one lost?

How can you differentiate?

Students who need scaffolding: Part of this game is the fun of choosing random students, but some students don't like that aspect. If you have students who need more time to prepare, give them a signal that they are next.

(If I put my hand on my head, that means after the person I call, it is you). Part of this game is also about having short reaction time. If you have students who need longer to react, give them that longer time. You don't need to give everyone the exact same amount of reaction time. Usually, students will not even notice.

Higher-level students: If students do well with this game, give them more difficult categories. Also, you can switch categories during the game. Example: Colors: Blue, green, red, yellow, (Teacher interrupts) "Yellow is also a word that starts with y, what are other 'y' words?" Game continues with that topic.

Link to Academics: *Content specific goals.* This game can be played in any content area. Come up with categories having to do with your unit. (Words that deal with photosynthesis, adjectives, words that have to do with adding).

Link to SEL: *Develop self-management skills.* This game involved people losing. It is a great opportunity to talk about how we react when we lose. What would happen if no one lost in any game? It would go on forever. Let the students do a "Reaction Walk" back to their desk. How fake sad can you be that you lost a game that doesn't matter? Talk to the students about what it feels like to lose, especially in front of other people. How can we cope with that feeling?

Link to Speaking and Listening: *General public speaking.* It can be difficult for some students to stand in front of their peers to present. This game is a good introduction to that since they just have to say one word. Remind students when they speak in front of an audience they must have good volume and eye contact.

*This game can be played by students who do not have any improv experience. It is a good game to use for a brain break or for a team building activity.

185

What ages? This game can be played with students in fifth grade and up. At younger grades, the point of this game is to show confidence. At older grades, the point of this game is to make puns and play with words.

What classes? This game is great for short transition times. It is also fun for morning meetings.

What is the goal? The goal of this game is to tell a joke. The joke does not have to be good (and sometimes it is even better when it is not).

How many people play? This is considered a line game where all students can play. In a show, actors would stand on stage in a line and step forward when they have a joke. In the classroom, you can either have the students line up and step out when they have a joke or just raise their hand.

How much time does it take? When teaching this game, it might take a little while to make sure that all students have had a chance to go. Once students understand how to play, the teacher can make this game as short or as long as needed.

What does the teacher do? The teacher gets suggestions from the audience. They might also need to change suggestions to make them more accessible. Example: The student gives a suggestion of a Dalmatian. The teacher changes it to a dog so there are more possibilities.

What do the other students do? While students are not playing, they are responsible for giving new suggestions when needed. I also usually introduce a cheer or something to do at the end of every joke (make a *ding* sound, say "Woo hoo!"). This makes it more interactive and supports all jokes, whether they make sense or not.

How do you play? This game relies on a standard setup of a joke: "185 _____ walk into Chili's (or another restaurant), the waitress says, "Sorry, we are closed", and then the students make a pun. If the suggestion is "banana", the joke could be "185 bananas walk into Chili's, the waitress says 'Sorry, we are closed,' so the bananas *split*." When this game is played in a show, the point is to make a real pun, but when playing it in class, the most important thing is for students to sell their joke. This means no matter how much the joke does not make sense, they stand and deliver it like it is the best joke they have ever told. I usually do an example to show the students, like, "185 bananas walk into Chili's, the waitress says, 'Sorry, we are closed,' so the bananas say, 'Well, I don't like you.'" I usually take a bow or pat myself on the back after. Show the students that the audience will still support them by doing your designated audience sound. Play goes for each suggestion until the teacher decides to get a new one. The teacher can go for as many suggestions as he or she wants.

How do you debrief? How did you feel when you had a good joke? How did you feel when you had a bad joke? How did *selling it* make you feel different? Audience members: What were the best jokes? How did you feel when people sold a bad joke? Can you still be entertained if the joke isn't funny?

How can you differentiate?

Students who need scaffolding: This game is a higher-level one. Some students just do not want to participate because there is a lot of pressure. If students do not want to play this game, I would not make them. They can be your helpers by giving suggestions, choosing people to give suggestions, or doing other specific noises as audience members. If you have students that want to participate but cannot grasp the pun portion of the game, have them purposefully tell jokes that don't make sense. Then, there is no pressure to come up with a joke and they still get the reaction from the crowd.

Higher-level students: Challenge your higher students to actually come up with puns. When I teach this game, I usually say to take the word and think of any other words they think are connected or related to it. Example: The word is dog: in my head I see the words puppy, poodle, K9, mutt, cat, ruff. Then I take one of those words and try to come up with a pun: "185 dogs walk into Chili's, the waiter says, 'Sorry, we are closed,' and the dogs say, 1. 'Man, that's ruff.' 2. 'We'll pay, we have K9 bucks.'" You could practice physically diagraming it on the board and then have them try some by themselves or in groups with a time limit.

Link to Academics: *Vocabulary acquisition and use.* Instead of playing this as a line game, change it to writing a joke book! Give students vocabulary words, concepts, people, and places from a unit. Tell them to come up with ten 185 jokes based on these concepts. Using the strategy of mapping out words related to the concept, students will automatically be reviewing the content that they learned through the unit.

Link to SEL: *Develop self-management skills.* This game is all about confidence. It can be really scary to stand up in front of other students and try to be funny. The beauty of this game is that students will get a great response from the audience whether the joke is great or not.

Link to Speaking and Listening: *Presentation of knowledge and ideas.* Kids (also me) tend to rush through the setup of the joke to get to the punchline. Talk to students about why it is important to speak slowly enough for the audience to understand.

*Once students know how to play this game, it is a great brain break or transition activity. It is also great during morning meetings or a closing circle.

Vacation Photos/ Night at the Museum

What ages? This game can be played at any grade.

What classes? This is a good game to play for fun, but also can be integrated into academic content areas easily such as science or social studies.

What is the goal? The skill worked on in this game is justification. Students will have to talk about a topic and then justify how a person's pose supports what they are talking about.

How many people play? There are two different roles in this game. The presenters are the people who tell the story, and the actors are the students who make poses on stage. I usually choose two students to work together to be presenters, but you could play with one student. For actors, I would choose between four and eight students, depending on your space.

How much time does it take? When I play this game, I usually give three rounds for the presenters to explain. You could easily do a round in less than five minutes. If you want everyone to get a turn, you will just need to do more than one round.

What does the teacher do? The teacher acts as the host. They get suggestions from the audience and lead the conversation with the students. They are also the one that tells the students in the back to 'freeze'.

What do the other students do? When students are not playing, they are acting as a good audience. They also should be thinking of new suggestions.

How do you play? Two students are brought to the front of the room as the presenters. Four to eight children are then chosen to be the actors. If you are playing this as Family Vacation, you get a location. If you want to play it as a museum, you get something you would like to see a museum about (yo-yos, cell phones). The teacher has the two presenters face the audience so they cannot see the people moving behind them. They then start to interview the students to find out information about either the vacation "Where did you go first?", or the museum "So, what is in the first room of the Cell Phone Museum?" Talk for a few seconds about what this picture is with the presenters' backs facing the other players. The teacher then yells "Freeze" and all the actors freeze in place. (This is also a good time to talk about keeping ourselves safe while playing: both feet on the ground, hands to ourselves.) The teacher has the presenters turn around and look at the other actors. Then, they have to justify what is happening in this picture. Example: Students are talking about their visit to the Cell Phone Museum. They have said that the first room has cell phone apps. When they turn around, they see a boy fake crying, someone asleep, and another one rocking a pretend baby. The presenters could explain that the person asleep is testing out the alarm app. The boy who is crying can't remember his Apple password, so he cannot restore all of his purchased apps, and the person with the baby is using Apple Music to play a lullaby for the baby. The game is to just always relate back to the topic. Once the students are done explaining the picture, you guide them to another room or another day on vacation. You can go as long or as short as you would like, but I usually do three pictures a round.

How do you debrief? First, talk to the actors about why they decided to make the poses they did. Were they listening to the presenters for ideas or were they just doing random movements? Which one is funnier? Then talk to the presenters about how they justified it. What were some that were easy, what were some that were hard?

How can you differentiate?

Students who need scaffolding: Most students will be able to be an actor in this scene. Some are more shy about it, and that is fine. Whatever pose they make is perfect. If a player has physical challenges, they can add noises or facial expressions. Students who still might struggle can be paired up with another student. There can also be modifications for students who might need more support in the presenter role. Make sure they have a good partner to work with. If they have a hard time coming up with things to say, assist them by asking questions with options or yes or no questions rather than open-ended ones. (Example: instead of saying "What did you do the next day?" you could ask, "The next day, did you go shopping or go swimming?" or "Did you like the museum?" Sometimes you can come up with follow-up questions based on the level of participation. The goal is always to have students participate as fully as they can, so if you have different levels of support for different students, that is fine.

Higher-level students: As the teacher, you can get more difficult topics for the students who are a higher-level. Example, instead of going to a place like Disney World for a vacation, you could request a place you would NOT like to go on vacation (dentist office, Wal-Mart). The students are still expected to present like it was the best vacation they have ever been on. If you have very advanced students, they can also take the role of interviewer from you.

Link to Academics: *Content area goals.* When playing Family Vacation, teachers can easily theme each round to meet the content that they are teaching. In science, we could take trips to different ecosystems or even inside the body. For history or social studies, the class could go back to a town in revolutionary times or on a trip around the White House.

Link to SEL: *Use social awareness and interpersonal skills.* This is a game that takes a partnership between the two presenters. They must accept what the other person says and add on to it. The teachers should point out how it feels when someone supports what you say and how you can support others.

Link to Speaking and Listening: *Presentation of ideas.* Presentations will be more common as students go through higher grades. Talk about what good presenters do.

Conducted Story

What ages? This game can be played with third graders and up. The younger the grade, the more scaffolding you will need to do.

What classes? This game is appropriate for academic classes in ELA and for community building in a homeroom setting or during morning meetings.

What is the goal? The goal of the game is to tell a story by working together. Students must only speak when it is their turn and be ready to jump into the story whenever the conductor chooses them.

How many people play? Each round of this game should have between three and six students. The game can be repeated as many times as you would like.

How much time does it take? The teacher controls when this game ends so they can monitor the time that is used to play. Usually, a round can be completed in less than five minutes.

What does the teacher do? The teacher gets the suggestion of the title of the story. They then control who starts the story, when they stop, and who continues. If the students need scaffolding or help, the teacher also needs to jump in and help the story keep going. Example: Teacher stops the student, saying, "Ok, now we are going to chapter 23, The Magic Forest."

What do the other students do? The other students act as good audience members. The teacher may also come to them at different points in the game to keep them engaged. Example: The story is called *The Little Chicken*. The teacher cuts off one of the students and decides to go to another chapter.

They then can turn to the audience and ask what animal should be introduced as a new character or where the next location should be.

How do you play? The teacher pulls three to six students to the front of the room. They then get a suggestion of a story that has never been written. I like to get titles by asking the audience for one word of the title at a time. This can easily turn into a review of parts of speech. "Give me an article (the). Give me an adjective (creepy). Now I need a noun (bike)". Now our story is called *The Creepy Bike*. Once the teacher chooses a title, they will explain to the students that only one person will be speaking at a time. When the teacher points at a student, that student starts telling the story. When the teacher wants that student to stop talking, they cut them off like a conductor does to an orchestra. Then, the teacher points to another student. This student must pick up exactly where the last student left off, be it at the end of a sentence or in the middle of a word. The teacher can jump around in the story, adding information or getting additional suggestions to integrate from the audience. The teacher usually ends the last chapter with "And the moral of the story is…" and has the students talk about what we should have learned from this chapter. You can repeat this process with as many new stories as you would like.

How do you debrief? Ask students what the easiest and hardest part was of this game. Why is listening so important? What happens if someone changed the story in a way you didn't expect?

How can you differentiate?

Students who need scaffolding: This game can be fast-paced. If you have students who are younger or have a harder time thinking on their feet, you can easily change this game to a version where students add one sentence at a time. You can have them start with the first person and then go down the line, everyone just adding one sentence. This way, students know when it is their turn to go. If you only have a few students who need scaffolding, try giving them a signal when they will be next, so they listen very closely. If the student still isn't sure what to say, ask a question, "Where do they go next?" or "What does he like to do for fun?" Only stay on this student for a short period of time, so they do not feel like they have to keep talking.

Higher-level students: This game can also be done as a competition. If you have students that are doing well, introduce the idea of eliminating them during the game. The teacher can call people out if they don't pick up exactly where the last person left off, don't make sense, or wait too long to respond.

Link to Academics: *Craft and structure, key idea and details.* This is a perfect game to integrate into ELA. A teacher could introduce different styles of writing (fables, myths, fairy tales) by explaining the different elements to them. Then, the students could play the game by making sure every step is represented in the specific style. This could also be a great way to talk about summarizing a story with a graphic organizer like: *Somebody, Wanted, But, Then, So.* Students could tell a story and then the class could work together to fill out the graphic organizer and write a complete summary.

Link to SEL: *Use interpersonal skills to maintain relationships.* Social stories are a big part of teaching social skills in classes. Think about a situation that has or might happen in your classroom: Bullying, bus issues, lack of taking turns. Start a story about a student who has these problems. The students will take turns telling this story just like the normal way of playing. However, the teacher can stop whenever they want and ask the audience if the action is a good idea or not. It can be turned into a "Choose Your Own Adventure" by having the audience vote on what the main characters should do next. Discussion can occur about what are good choices and what are bad choices in this situation and what can happen due to these choices.

Link to Speaking and Listening: *Comprehension and Collaboration.* Students will need to listen actively to each other to make sure they continue the story. For older/more advanced students, the teacher could do eliminations based on students not repeating what was said before, but just naturally going in. Example: if one student said, "And then the boy said," and then the next person repeats, "The boy said," they would be out.

Gibberish Expert

What ages? This game would be best for students in sixth grade and up.

What classes? This game lends itself well to academic areas such as science, social studies, music, art, or physical education. There are fewer students involved in the actual playing of this game, so I would not use it as a brain break or during morning meeting/closing circle.

What is the goal? The goal of this game is to use gibberish and gestures to help communicate ideas and emotions.

How many people play? In the most common version of this game, only two students would play at a time. One would be the *Expert* and one would be the *Translator*. To get more students participating at a time, I would choose three *Experts* and three *Translators*.

How much time does it take? This game takes a little bit more time to set up and to play. I would leave at least ten minutes to play one round.

What does the teacher do? The teacher acts as the host, leading the conversation and getting questions from the audience.

What do the other students do? The students that are not acting as an *Expert* or *Translator* act as a good audience. They also are the ones that need to come up with questions.

How do you play? One student acts as an expert in a field. Unfortunately, they only speak a made-up language of gibberish. Another student acts as a translator who can speak both English and gibberish. After an area is chosen (volleyball, chemistry, YouTube) audience members ask questions of the expert. The translator must speak gibberish (made-up syllables) to the expert who then answers the question with gibberish to the translator, who then relays the answer to the audience in English. The expert must rely on their voice, body language, and gestures to get ideas across. There are no right or wrong answers. The game goes as long as the teacher would like.

How do you debrief? As the expert, how could you communicate with the translator? Were you able to give clues and communicate in any other way than the words? How did your voice pitch, tone, and volume change with different answers?

How can you differentiate?

Students who need scaffolding: This game can be hard for students. Give students who need help a fellow translator or a fellow expert to guide them. Students who are less confident would be better suited to playing the expert because that person doesn't actually have to *speak* in front of the class. They get to simply use gibberish to answer the questions. The translator is the one who has the hardest work for this game.

Higher-level students: If students are able to play the basics of the game, tell them to explore how to get more out of their gibberish and body language. Tell them to add emotion to their answer or do more bantering between experts and translators.

Link to Academics: *Content specific goals.* This game can be fun at either the beginning of a unit to introduce topics or at the end to review. Have the expert be knowledgeable in a topic that your class just studied (soccer, the northwest region). Challenge the students to find a way to really answer the questions with correct answers.

Link to SEL: *Using interpersonal skills.* This game highlights how much information you can share without saying a word. Talk to the students about how you can tell what someone is feeling without them having to talk. What other ways can you communicate feelings?

Link to Speaking and Listening: *Comprehension and collaboration.* This game has a set of rules for how to communicate. Students must follow this structure in order for the game to be successful. Talk to students about how there are times where we need to have structure to make a presentation or collaboration successful.

Exaggeration Station

What ages? This game is best played for younger students, fifth grade and below. However, older students can also play this game as a quick warm-up.

What classes? This game is a fun brain break. It is also great to play during morning meetings or closing circles.

What is the goal? The goal of this game is to practice reacting in big ways. Students will have to think of how to express different emotions through facial expressions and body language.

How many people play? This game is played by the whole class at the same time.

How much time does it take? The teacher controls the amount of time this game takes. It can be played where every student gets to say a comment while others react. In that case, it should take around five minutes. The game can also be broken into short segments to play during a brain break or transition, and in that case, only a few students give comments.

What does the teacher do? The teacher calls on students and does a countdown while the students react.

What do the other students do? All students play every round.

How do you play? One student is chosen to make a statement. This should be something neutral that should not evoke emotion. Examples: "The sky is blue." "I have three pencils in my bag." When the other students hear the statement, they have to react in a way that they normally would not react, at 100%. For example, if a student said, "I got a haircut yesterday." one student might choose to react by pretending to cry, another by jumping up and down with joy. The teacher counts down from 5 while the students act in their chosen emotions. Once the teacher is done counting, the students go back to neutral. The teacher then picks another student to make a statement. This cycle continues until everyone has gotten a chance to make a statement or as long as the teacher wants.

How do you debrief? Start a conversation about different emotions and how you can use facial expressions and body language to show them. Talk about what it felt like to overreact to something. Ask students how it felt to react to something that didn't deserve that reaction.

How can you differentiate?

Students who need scaffolding: Most students are able to participate in this game fully. If a student has a hard time coming up with a statement, ask them a question: "Zeke, tell me what color my shirt is." "What is on your desk?" Make sure they say the answer in a full sentence, and restate the question. If you have students who have a hard time choosing an emotion, have a few written on the board before the game. The class can participate in this brainstorming session. They can use one of those if they don't know what else to do. You can also buddy up students who might need help with other students who know how to play. Then when it's time to react, the student who might need help has a model to watch.

Higher-level students: If students are doing well with this game, make them give their neutral statements in gibberish. This is a made-up language that doesn't make sense. After the other students hear the gibberish, they react in the same way.

Link to Academics: *Content area curriculum.* This could be a fun game to play during an introduction or review of a unit. Students could go around making statements of something that they have learned during the unit and others can react in strong ways to each statement. This activity could also be integrated into a KWL chart. Students could take time to preview a unit, coming up with things they know or want to know. After sharing these with the class, students could do a large reaction to the statement (if you already know it: be thrilled, if you don't know anything about a statement, be upset.)

Link to SEL: *Developing self-awareness.* This is a great lesson to link to overreacting. After playing this game, talk about how in improv and acting, we like to play at 100% emotion. However, in real life, we usually don't react at 100%. Write some scenarios on the board. Examples: I fell down. I got an A on a test. My friend didn't want to play with me. Lead students through a conversation about what emotions they would feel, how they would act, and what percentage they would show.

Link to Speaking and Listening: *Presentation of ideas.* When people are overreacting, it can be hard to understand them. Discuss with students that this game is an exaggeration, and during presentations, you need to speak clearly and calmly.

Spelling Bee

What ages? This game is best for older students, usually sixth grade and above. But depending on your group of children, you could also have fourth and fifth graders play this game.

What classes? This is a fun game to integrate into any class with vocabulary words.

What is the goal? The goal of the game is to work as a team to spell words one letter at a time. The goal is to spell the word correctly (because let me say, there is nothing like it when a group actually spells a word correctly). However, the ultimate goal is to work as a team to keep the tempo of the game flowing. The team should listen and respond quickly.

How many people play? This is a game that is played in groups. Originally, the game was intended to have three players. However, you can have up to five students, depending on how you need to group.

How much time does it take? This game takes a little bit of time, probably at least 5 minutes per round. If you want to make sure that everyone gets a turn, be sure to leave a good amount of time. However, if you are not worried about having all of the students participate, you can do one or two rounds to fit the time that you have.

What does the teacher do? The teacher acts as the host of the spelling competition. They keep the game going and step in when side coaching is needed. They also gather the word suggestions from the audience.

What do the other students do? The other students act as the audience members and come up with suggestions.

How do you play? The teacher introduces the spelling team and gives them a word to spell for practice. The teacher should make this word grade level appropriate. Examples: *school, puppy, science.* The students all repeat the word one time and take a bow, altogether, as one person. Then, the students start spelling the word taking turns adding one letter at a time. (This might take some directions from the teacher at first, but after a while, the students tend to catch on.) When the students have finished the word (or you help them signal that the word is over) they take a bow as a group. Option 1: For younger grades, only have them spell the words. Once the group has finished, get a new word. Encourage the audience to start with first grade level words and get harder as the game progresses. Option 2: For older students, have them use the word in a sentence created by adding one word at a time. After the group spells the word and creates a sentence, the teacher will get another word.

How do you debrief? Ask the students what was challenging. What happened if someone in front of you said a letter you didn't think they would say? If you knew you were wrong, did that change your level of confidence? What should you do if you actually know how to spell the word, but someone else gave the wrong letter? If that happened, how did you feel? For more advanced students making sentences, how did you decide what to say in the sentence? Did it make sense altogether?

How can you differentiate?

Students who need scaffolding: I would always start this game with just spelling the word. Students who need more help can usually participate at this level.

Higher-level students: Challenge the students to make a sentence that tells us the definition of the word. This way, they are reviewing what the vocabulary word means as well as playing the game.

Link to Academics: *Vocabulary acquisition and use.* This game can be an introduction to vocabulary words. The teacher can give the word and a definition and then the students can try to spell it. Older/more advanced students can also try to use it in a sentence. An example of this could be if you are starting a science unit on different types of animals. The teacher could give the students the word mammal, the definition, and then have them spell it and use it in a sentence one word at a time.

Link to SEL: *Use interpersonal skills.* In this game, students must work together to have any success. Talk about how active listening and agreeing with your partners help in situations where you must work in a group.

Link to Speaking and Listening: *Presentation of ideas.* Students will need to listen very carefully to all other players to make sure the word that they contribute makes sense.

Wrong Jeopardy

What ages? I have used this exercise with students in grades three and above.

What classes? This game works great in any class, especially in the beginning of the year. Throughout the year, you can also play it when you have a few extra minutes.

What is the goal? The goal of this game is to teach children they should not be scared of being wrong. One of the biggest challenges in education is to make students feel comfortable taking risks in front of each other. Throughout the year, we expect students to feel comfortable failing, but rarely do we let them experience the feeling of failure in a safe space.

How many people play? In the classic game, there are three contestants per round. I have played it with up to five, and it works well.

How much time does it take? Each round takes around five minutes, depending on the number and level of people playing.

What does the teacher do? The teacher acts as the host. She gets questions from the audience and runs the game.

What do the other students do? The other students act as the audience giving suggestions. They need to be prepared to act as a good audience.

How do you play? The teacher picks the players and they stand in front of the audience. The teacher introduces the show and explains how this is the smartest group of people in the word. She then has each student make a *ring in* sound and introduce themselves. Students are encouraged to come up with a character that seems very smart. Example: "(rings in) Hello, my name is Dr. Elizabeth Smith. I have my law degree from Harvard and have never had a B in my life." "My name is Ben Green and I am an actual brain surgeon. I also design computers in my free time." The host gets questions that have one right answer that kindergarten students would know the answer to and asks them to the contestants. Students ring in when they know the answer. They will answer the questions as incorrectly as possible. The teacher will react to the wrong answers and then at the end of each round, tell the correct answer. Rounds can last 3-5 questions, depending on the time limit.

How do you debrief? After each round, ask the contestants what it felt like to be wrong in front of their peers. Most of the time, the students will say it was "funny." Ask them if they are still alive and if the world is still spinning. They will say "yes." Then ask the audience what they thought. Ask if they think any less of the people who answered incorrectly. Remind the students they will never be more wrong in front of their peers. If they can survive this, they can survive taking risks and possibly being wrong in class.

How can you differentiate?

Students who need scaffolding: The first rule to tell students is that they will never be forced to participate. I have had many students who have said they don't want to play change their minds once they see the audience reaction. Students who do not want to play may often not have an idea of what to say. Some helpful things to suggest to the students would be: "Look around the room and say something you see." "What is the opposite of the right number?" "What is something that starts with the same letter as the right answer?"

Higher-level students: Encourage people to make puns. If the question is, "What is two plus two?" and the students know it is four, they can give an answer that rhymes with four. "Well... OBVIOUSLY, the answer is door."

Students can also lean into characters by using accents, body language, or both.

Link to Academics: *Content area goals.* This game could be played at the beginning or the ending of a unit. Questions about a certain topic could be asked and after the players get the questions wrong, someone in the audience could give the actual answer. If this game is played at the beginning of a unit, a KWL chart could be started with the questions given, with the answers being filled in as the unit continues.

Link to SEL: *Develop self-awareness.* This game is all about confidence. I like playing this game at the beginning of the year. After each round, I ask the students how they feel. Usually they say it was fun. I ask them to check and see if the earth has swallowed them whole? They will say no. This is as wrong as these children will be in front of their peers. The students will never be as wrong as they just were, so they should have no fear of answering a question wrong or asking a question in front of this group of students now.

Link to Speaking and Listening: *Presentation of knowledge and ideas.* Students need to speak clearly and loudly enough in this game. Talk to the children about how they can show confidence through their voice.

Reporter
on the Street

What ages? This game works best for students who have done some acting work before (developing character, listening skills). Because of that, I would suggest using this game for students in grades six and above. However, if you have more advanced students, feel free to use it.

What classes? This game can be used on its own for homeroom, morning meeting, or advisory to just have fun. It can also be used as a tool for point of view in a content area such as reading, science, or social studies. Instead of making up a random event, you would use something in an area you are learning about. Examples: a chapter in the novel *Holes* you are reading in a book club, the years of the United States Revolutionary War you are studying in social studies, or the parts of a flower you are studying in science.

What is the goal? The goal is to have students take turns asking and answering questions. Students will take turns being reporters and witnesses to an event. The students will get to explore characters and answer questions from a different point of view.

How many people play? I would do one to two reporters at a time working with four to seven witnesses. If you would like everyone to have a turn, you can just do another round.

How much time does it take? Each round can last between five to ten minutes, depending on how many students are involved. You can make it last longer if each witness gets more than one question or reporters go back for follow up. If you are short on time, you will need to limit questions and guide students to move on to other witnesses.

What does the teacher do? The teacher acts as the news anchor who interrupts the TV show the class is watching with "breaking news." The teacher also is the moderator and keeps the flow of the interviews going. The teacher may need to give directions: "I see a witness in a blue shirt, can you go talk to this person?" or you may need to feed the reporters questions. The anchor will be the one watching the clock, so they can set the pace.

What do the other students do? Once the suggestion is given, the rest of the students act as the audience. Remember to go over what makes a good audience member before you start.

How do you play? If you are playing this game for fun instead of for academics, you will get a suggestion of either a really boring news story (Mrs. W is wearing a blue shirt today) or something that could never happen (Dogs have started driving cars). The teacher will start the game by saying something like, "Good evening, we are sorry to interrupt your viewing of *Watching Paint Dry and Other Extreme Sports*, but we have breaking news for you!" They then will start talking to the reporter or reporters. Let them introduce themselves and maybe ask a basic question. ("What in the world is going on out there?") After they seem comfortable, send them around the classroom to the designated witnesses. These witnesses can either stay seated in their desk or be placed around the room. (Sometimes it is funnier if they are in different positions around the room already acting before the reporter comes over to them). The reporter walks around and asks questions to the witnesses about the event ("When did you first see the dogs driving?" "What kind of dogs have you seen?" "How has this affected you?") Remind the students to use open-ended questions, usually ones that start with who, what, when, where, why, or how. When the witnesses have all been interviewed, the anchor wraps up the segment and sends it back to the regular show.

How do you debrief? Once the game is over, start with the reporters and ask them how it felt to be leading the interviews. Was it easy, hard? What kind of questions did you use? Then, talk to the people being interviewed. Ask them how they found their character and how it felt to be interviewed. Ask students what it felt like to take on another point of view.

How can you differentiate?

Students that need scaffolding: You could assign characters before the game begins. Example: If you are reading the novel *Holes*, you could assign characters to the players: The Warden, Stanley, Zero. You could also allow teams of two if you have students who do not feel comfortable being interviewed alone. As the anchor, you also have the power to restate the question in easier terms. If the reporter asks, "How do you feel about dogs driving cars?" and the witness freezes, you could rephrase it to something like, "Were you scared when you saw the dogs driving cars?" It is more fun to ask open-ended questions, but some students need more structure.

Higher-level students: If you feel like you will not need to control the time or pacing of the game, you can let a student act as the anchor. You also can transform this game to a version of a talk show. Characters then can interact more and talk about their emotions and feelings toward each other.

Link to Academics: *Content area goals, key ideas and details.* This game can be integrated into content areas like science or social studies. You can have the reporters visit a certain place like Boston during the Revolutionary War or a desert biome.

Link to SEL: *Use interpersonal skills to maintain relationships.* This game is about putting yourself in other people's shoes. Talk about how a group of people can be involved in the same situation but have different points of view. Is there one right point of view?

Link to Speaking and Listening: *Comprehension and collaboration.* This game involves interviewing. Talk to students about how to interview others and actively listen to have a follow-up question. Also talk to students about staying on topic when being interviewed.

Magic Elevator

What ages? This game is best used for students in second grade and below, but any age can play.

What classes? This can be integrated into any class, especially morning meetings.

What is the goal? The goal of this game is to have students act out different situations and react with their body and facial expressions.

How many people play? One student suggests a place and another student suggests a floor number per round, but the rest of the class also participates.

How much time does it take? This game takes less than thirty seconds per round. If you want to give everyone a chance to give a suggestion, it will take about ten minutes. If you want to just do a few, you could be done in a few minutes.

What does the teacher do? The teacher chooses who will be giving the suggestion. They also do the countdown for how long the children act out each scenario.

What do the other students do? Everyone plays each round.

How do you play? The teacher tells students to pick an environment. This can include many things: actual places (forest, Antarctica, a trampoline park) or a substance (water, Jello, peanut butter). The student picks a random number for the floor. The teacher announces, "Floor 34, the land of peanut butter." The students act like they are in a place full of peanut butter. The teacher counts down from 10 while the students are acting. When the time is up, the teacher gives the cue (rings a bell, claps hands) to signal the round is over. Continue with as many other rounds as wanted.

How do you debrief? Ask the students to describe how they reacted to different scenarios. Comment on different ways that they walked and why they acted the ways they did. What is easier to walk through, mud or Jello? How would your face look interacting with different environments?

How can you differentiate?

Students that need scaffolding: If you know there are students that are going to struggle, have a basket full of suggestions that they can pull from. That way, students can still participate, but won't have the pressure to come up with a scenario. Also, students can be put into pairs if there are ones that have difficulty deciding how to react.

Higher-level students: Challenge higher-level students to not only pick more interesting places, but to also have more exaggerated reactions. Remember to not only react with your body, but also with your facial expressions. Would your speech change in different environments? What would you do with your hands?

Link to SEL: *Use social-awareness skills.* Lots of emotions are shown through facial expressions. Tell students to focus on looking at each others' faces during this game. How can you show through your face if you are having an easy or a hard time doing something?

Link to Academics: *Demonstrate command of conventions of English grammar, content area goals.* This game could easily be integrated into a lesson about adjectives and adverbs. Pick locations and have students describe what the location is like (hot, cold, big, small) and how they walked (slowly, quickly). Make a list on the board of adjectives and adverbs. This game could also be used when learning about different environments in geography. Walk through the Savannah, walk through the Arctic. Make a list on the board of what you see and how you acted.

Red Ball

What ages? This game can be used with students of all ages.

What classes? This game can be played quickly and anywhere. It is a great energizer as well as a listening activity. You can also integrate pretty much any content areas in the game.

What is the goal? There are two major goals of this game: reinforcing the idea of *Yes, and,* and listening to each other.

How many people play? This is a good game to play as a whole group. I have played with over 20 people, and I have also played with groups as small as 5-6. The game feels different with larger and smaller groups, but the goals stay the same.

How much time does it take? This is one of the short improv games. If you have younger children, I usually encourage making sure everyone gets a turn, so it might take a little longer the first few times. For older students who have played before, you can do this in less than five minutes.

What does the teacher do? The teacher introduces the concept and usually introduces each new item. They make sure that the game is flowing. Once this game is played more than once, a student can usually be placed in charge of running this game.

What do the other students do? All students play this game at the same time.

How do you play? The teacher reaches into their pocket or a bag. They pull out a pretend red ball and show everyone. This is the time to reinforce "Yes, and." Make sure that the students all 'see' that you have a red ball in your hand. Pick a student to throw the ball to. You get the student's eye contact, say the student's name, throw the 'ball' and say, "Red Ball" after it. When the student catches the ball, they say "Thank you, Red Ball." That student then chooses another student to throw the ball to, following the pattern of "Student name, Red Ball". That student then says, "Thank you, Red Ball". The first time students play this game, have everyone raise their hands until they have gotten the red ball. Each time you play, try to go quicker. Once the students understand how the game works, the teacher then introduces a yellow ball. Start the red ball over again and then introduce the yellow ball once the red ball is going well. You can add in more as you see fit. The game ends with the teacher taking back the red ball and putting it away.

How do you debrief? Ask the students what they had to do to make sure the ball kept getting passed around. Hopefully, they will talk about speaking clearly and loudly and making sure that they have the attention of the person who they are throwing it to. Ask students how they can communicate without saying words. Make sure to talk about eye contact and having your body facing the person you are throwing it to.

How can you differentiate?

Students who need scaffolding: Practice the exact steps before the game is played. Role-play step-by-step with students who need extra support. If they still need assistance, talk them through the steps once they catch the ball. I have had to do this many times, and honestly, it does not affect the flow of the game. After a few times, they usually catch on.

Higher-level students: Let the students come up with sillier things to throw. One of my kids' favorites is 'cow'. Talk to students about how you act differently if you are catching a ball versus something heavy like a cow.

Think about how things feel, how much they weigh, and what they smell like. Think about how you would transport things from one person to another. You would move a bowling ball differently than you would move a feather.

Link to Academics: *Conventions of grammar, vocabulary, content area goals.* This game can be integrated into many academic areas. You can throw items that are described by adjectives (slippery, furry, heavy, metallic). You can also throw different items that you are learning about. Maybe you are learning about different animals. How would dessert animals get from one person to another? Would one run and another one fly? How could you act that out?

Link to SEL: *Use social-awareness and self-management skills.* This game is all about *Yes, and.* Students must support each other in the idea that a red ball is being thrown around. If one person isn't in on the game, the game ends. Talk to students about why it is important to support each other and how it feels when people say *Yes, and* to ideas.

Link to Speaking and Listening: *Presentation of ideas.* It can be a struggle to encourage children to make eye contact with each other. This game makes it fun and necessary to be successful. They only need to make eye contact for a short period of time, so it is a good way to build that skill.

Yes, Let's!

What ages? This game is appropriate for any age, but it is best for fifth grade and below. You can make it more challenging for older students as well.

What classes? This game is great for team building in morning meetings or homeroom, but can also be integrated into content area classes.

What is the goal? The goal of this game is to encourage students to embrace *Yes, and.* Students will get to see how it feels to accept a suggestion that others have given as well as what it feels like for others to accept their offer.

How many people play? This game involves everyone in the class. Make sure that the students are spread throughout the classroom so they have room to play.

How much time does it take? This game can take as little or as long as the teacher would like. For younger students, I usually make sure the first time we play, everybody gets to give a suggestion, so it takes longer. Once you have played once, each game does not have to include everyone giving suggestions.

What does the teacher do? The teacher acts as the director, choosing children to give suggestions. They also encourage and side-coach the students as they participate.

What do the other students do? All students play during this game.

How do you play? One student is chosen to give an action. This could be something basic like walking or jumping or acting out something else through mime, like skydiving or scuba diving. The students walk around the space and when the child who is giving the suggestions is ready, they say "Hey, everybody! Let's (action)". All of the other students say back "Yes! Let's," and begin to silently do that activity. When the student who has given the suggestions has gotten to see everyone acting, they say "Thank you." At this signal, everyone starts walking normally around the space again until another student is chosen to give a suggestion. The first time the teacher plays this game, they should make sure that everyone gets a chance to give a suggestion.

How do you debrief? After the game is over, ask someone how it felt for the other students to say "Yes, Let's" to their idea. Did you feel supported? Did it feel good that people were agreeing with you? Then ask what would have happened if everyone said "NO!" and refused to play? Would we have had a game? Ask students to explain how they felt acting the suggestions out. Were any harder than others? Did you feel silly doing any of them? How did you get over the feeling of being silly? Did it help to know others were being silly with you?

How can you differentiate?

Students who need scaffolding: The teacher can have suggestions in a bowl that students can pull from if they feel pressure to come up with an activity. The teacher can also coach students by asking questions like, "What do you like to do outside?" or, "What did you do in the gym today?"

Higher-level students: Give students a category to pick an activity from (sports, act like an animal). Teachers can also encourage students to use gibberish to give activities like "Hey everybody, Let's schubba shub." No one knows what this is, so the students are free to decide what that means in their head and act that way.

Link to Academics: *Conventions of English grammar, vocabulary, content area goals* This game is a great lesson when learning about verbs. Teachers can also integrate this into a social studies or science lesson based on a location. "Think of things you can do in the rainforest." "What about ancient Egypt?"

Link to SEL: *Develop interpersonal skills.* During this game, players need to have faith that others will follow along. Ask the students what it feels like when everyone shouts 'Yes, Let's!' How can we bring that energy into our day-to-day classes?

Index of Suggestions

Jobs

Teacher	Dolphin Trainer	Musician	Fire Fighter
Professor	Computer Engineer	Makeup Artist	Bank Teller
Reporter	Party Planner	Baker	Magician
Artist	Chemist	Lawyer	Carpenter
Doctor	Forklift Driver	Pilot	Archaeologist

Objects

Stapler	Duck	Shooting Star	Marker
Kite	Giraffe	Bike	Cup of Coffee
Guitar	Frying Pan	Fly Swatter	Rocking Chair
Computer	Chopsticks	Potato	Duct Tape
Bottle of Perfume	Toothpaste	Mop	Candy Cane

Emotions

Love	Envy	Excitement	Gratitude
Happiness	Hungry	Pained	Frightened
Scared	Surprised	Rage	Joyful
Bored	Despair	Hatred	Optimistic
Disappointed	Upset	Proud	Overwhelmed

Characteristics

Speaks like a pirate	Giggles all the time	You have a secret	Running for mayor
Professional Wrestler	Owns 100 cats	Collects bugs	Is overly helpful
Only whispers	Really rich	Afraid of everything	Is actually an animal
Is very confident	Poet	Always exercising	Speaks properly all of the time
99 years old	4 years old	From the past	From the future

Voices

Quiet	Loud (not yelling)	Sounds like royalty	Opera singer
Rapper	New Anchor	Speaks quickly	Speaks slowly
High Pitch	Low Pitch	100 years old	Baby
Cartoon Character	College Professor	Animal of your choice	Bad cold (stuffed up)

Things with instruction manuals

Spaceship	Computer	Car	House
Guitar	Bike	Microwave	Refrigerator
Motorcycle	X-Ray Machine	Time Machine	Roller Coaster
Train	Helicopter	Soccer Ball	Air Conditioner
Video Game	Legos	IKEA Desk	3D Printer

Open-ended questions

Why did the chicken cross the road?

Why is the sky blue?

How do you make a Thanksgiving dinner?

How do you travel to space?

Why do people wash their hands?

What is the difference between adding and subtracting?

What is the best way to build a house?

Why is reading important?

What happens when you mix all of the colors together?

Why is a baby goat called a kid?

Questions with correct answers

What is two plus two?	How do you spell cat?
What color do you get when you put blue and yellow together?	What country are we in?
What planet are we on?	What animal says "moo"?
How many eyes do you have?	What letter comes after A?
What does T-H-E spell?	What is the opposite of up?

Actions/Activities

Hitting a baseball	Serving a volleyball	Painting a fence	Making bread
Mowing the lawn	Washing a window	Playing tennis	Playing with slime
Swimming	Running	Climbing a ladder	Playing the drums
Playing a guitar	Doing yoga	Roller skating	Skiing

Categories

Colors	States	Foods	Fruits
Movies	TV Shows	Pieces of clothing	Types of chips
Pets	Zoo animals	Countries	Things in a classroom
Types of candy	Things you eat for dinner	Things in a park	Sports
Vegetables	Toys	Holidays	Songs

Names of stories that have never been written

The Most Beautiful Chipmunk

A Trip to Jupiter

The Baby Who Ran the World

Jeff's Trip to the Mountain

A Star for Julie

The Dolphin Picnic

Gee, I Love Cheese

My Favorite Alien

Cats and More Cats

The Dog That Won
the Lottery

Spelling words

cat	dog	bird	yard
child	bread	pretty	America
beautiful	friendship	wonderful	photosynthesis
onomatopoeia	orange	turtle	biology
a	gnome	gorilla	tortilla

Boring News Story

A dog barked at a cat

A leaf fell from a tree

The coffee fell on the ground

It is raining outside

Someone found a dollar on
the ground

The restaurant is out of soup

The teacher is wearing
black shoes

Someone ate the last cookie

The balloon ran out of air

The milk went bad

Locations

Top of a mountain	Grocery store	White House	Museum
Bank	Coffee shop	Mansion	Antarctica
Inside a volcano	In space	Toy store	Garden
Beach	Restaurant	Hospital	Gas station
Train station	Desert	Zoo	Library

Works Cited

Aladesuyi, Oluwakemi, and Audrey Nguyen. "The Rules of Improv Can Make You Funnier. They Can Also Make You More Confident." *NPR LifeKit*, 29 Nov. 2022, www.npr.org/2022/10/19/1129907651/ improv-can-build-confidence-heres-how-to-apply-it-to-your-everyday-life?utm_campaign=storyshare&utm_source=facebook. com&utm_medium=social&fbclid=IwAR2m_yO1eNHy6D1cPs1_ HrXO1SyaxKar3rbGiHsbz8nsUwm8y5cSMjlMUFw. Accessed 26 Apr. 2023.

Common Core State Standards Initiative. *English Language Arts & Literacy in History/Social Studies, Science, and Technical Subjects.* learning. ccsso.org/wp-content/uploads/2022/11/ELA_Standards1.pdf. Accessed 7 Apr. 2023.

Council of Chief State School Officers. "ELA Standards." *Common Core State Standards*, Common Core State Standards Initiative, learning.ccsso.org/ wp-content/uploads/2022/11/ELA_Standards1.pdf. Accessed 26 Apr. 2023.

Graziadio Staff. "What Are Soft Skills in Business? | Pepperdine Graziadio Business School." *Bschool.pepperdine.edu*, 7 Jan. 2020, bschool.pepperdine.edu/blog/posts/soft-skills-business.htm.

Illinois State Board of Education. "Social Emotional Learning Standards." *SEL-Standards*, www.isbe.net/Documents/SEL-Standards.pdf. Accessed 26 Apr. 2023.

Responsive Classroom. "About Responsive Classroom | Responsive Classroom." *Responsive Classroom*, 2019, www.responsiveclassroom.org/ about/.